THE BOARD MEMBER'S BOOK

Making a Difference in Voluntary Organizations

Third Edition

BRIAN O'CONNELL

THE FOUNDATION CENTER

Also by Brian O'Connell

America's Voluntary Spirit
Board Overboard: Laughs and Lessons For All But the Perfect Nonprofit
Civil Society: The Underpinnings of America Democracy
Effective Leadership in Voluntary Organizations
People Power: Service Advocacy, Enpowerment
Philanthropy in Action
Powered by Coalition: The Story of INDEPENDENT SECTOR
Values
Voices from the Heart: In Celebration of America's Volunteers
Volunterrs in Action (with Ann Brown O'Connell)

Library of Congress Cataloging-in-Publication Data
O'Connell, Brian, 1930-
   The board member's book: making a difference in voluntary
organizations / Brian O'Connell.— 3rd ed.
        p. cm.
Includes bibliographical references (p.) and index.
   ISBN 1-931923-17-5 (paperback : alk. paper)
   1.   Endowments—United States—Officials and employees. 2.
Voluntarism—United States. I. Title.
   HV97.A3O33 2003
   361.7'632'068—dc21

                                                            2003007684

This book is dedicated to the board members
of America's voluntary organizations.

It is to you who make the difference for so many
Important causes, and it is you who build the
caring spirit of our society

Contents

Part III: Appendixes

Foreword

This book is dedicated to the board members of America's voluntary organizations. It is also written for the—to try to match their spirit and determination with some hard-won lessons from fifty years as a community organizer.

Board members can make an enormous difference for organizations, causes, and crusades. Much of the progress of America is testimony to the power of what Richard Carter calls "the gentle legions."

Board membership can also be agonizingly ineffective and disheartening. People care passionately about causes or institutions, and they want the best for them, but human institutions are all less than perfect, and voluntary organizations in particular can require more interaction than most of us can bear. This book begins with the observation that "people who get involved with public causes open themselves to frustration and disappointment. . . .," but it goes on to make the much more important point that ". . .through it all and after it all— those moments of making change happen for the better are among our lasting joys. There is something wonderfully rewarding in being part of an effort that makes a difference."

The book is an attempt to talk to board members who want to make the most of their volunteer efforts. I want to assure them that they can make a tremendous difference for their causes and organizations.

Part I attempts to make clear the impact of volunteers and voluntary organizations. Part II, the body of the book, talks about the effectiveness of boards and board members in planning, evaluation, fundraising, and in their many other essential functions. Part III provides some detail on selected topics and includes the usual reference list and index. It also includes something just for the fun of it. Because volunteering should be fun as well as inspirational and effective, I've added "Minutes of Our Last Meeting," which I hope provides a lighter moment. Indeed, I have tried hard to give the whole book an upbeat tone to go along with what should be the positive character of voluntary effort.

Most of all, I've tried to make it the board member's book.

Acknowledgment and appreciation are extended once again to several funders whose support helped make possible the first and second editions of this book, including the Durfee, George Gund, Packard, Premier Industrial, 3M, and Wells Fargo foundations. This third edition was helped greatly by support of my current work from Atlantic Philanthropies, Inc., Carnegie Corporation of New York, Charles Stewart Mott Foundation, and Rockefeller Brothers Fund.

Tom Buckman, retired president of the Foundation Center, and Pat Read, former director of Editorial Services and editor of the first edition of this book, were wonderfully encouraging and helpful. Their successors, Sara Engelhardt and Rick Schoff, have been equally supportive of the second and now this third edition.

For this time around Sharon Stewart served remarkably as research and editorial assistant and Mary Perry equally as general assistant. The book and I owe a great deal to both of them.

With acknowledgment and appreciation,

Brian O'Connell
Chatham, Massachusetts
August 2002

Part I

The Power of Volunteers and Voluntary Organizations

1

The Personal Meaning of Volunteering

People who get involved with public causes open themselves to frustration and disappointment, but—through it all and after it all—those moments of making change happen for the better are among our lasting joys. There's something wonderfully rewarding in being part of an effort that makes a difference. And there's something rewarding in being among other people when they're at their best too.

When we take inventory of the meaning of our lives, these special experiences have to be among the high points. Happiness is, in the end, a simple thing. Despite how complicated we try to make it or the entrapments we substitute for it, happiness is caring and being able to do something about it.

In the community sense, caring and service are giving and volunteering. As far back as the twelfth century, the highest order and benefit of charity was described by Maimonides in the Mishna Torah: "The highest degree, than which there is nothing higher, is to take hold of a Jew who has been crushed and to give him a gift or a loan or to enter into partnership with him or to find work for him, and then to put him on his feet so he will not be dependent on his fellow man."

In a world just sixty years removed from the slaughter of six million Jews, and still rampant with diseases and other indignities of the vilest form and breadth, there is room for concern and caring, for charity and volunteering. Indeed, in this still young democracy, there is total dependence on citizen determination to preserve the freedoms so recently declared and to extend them to all.

The problems of contemporary society are more complex, the solutions more involved, and the satisfactions more obscure, but the basic ingredients are still the caring and the resolve to make things better. From the simplicity of these have come today's exciting efforts on behalf of humanitarian causes ranging from equality to environment and from health to peace.

In the course of these efforts, there is at work a silent cycle of cause and effect that I call the "genius of fulfillment," that is, the harder people work for others and for the fulfillment of important social goals, the more fulfilled they are themselves. Confucius expressed it by saying, "Goodness is God," meaning that the more good we do, the happier we are, and the totality of it all is a supreme state of being. Thus, he said, God is not only a Supreme Being apart from us, but a supreme state of being within us.

Aristotle, too, caught an important part of it when he said, "Happiness is the utilization of one's talents along lines of excellence."

A simpler way of looking at the meaning of service is a quotation from an epitaph:

> What I spent is gone
> What I kept is lost
> But what I gave to charity
> Will be mine forever.

How we express the meaning of service doesn't really matter. It can be charity or enlightened self-interest or simply humanity to other people. These are all ways of describing why we volunteer, why volunteering provides some of our happiest moments, and why the good that we do lives after us.

2

The Impact of Volunteers and Voluntary Organizations

The United States is the only country in the world where giving and volunteering are pervasive characteristics of the total society. In his introduction to my book, *America's Voluntary Spirit,* John W. Gardner wrote, "Virtually every significant social idea in this country has been nurtured in the nonprofit sector."

Think back to the sources of ideas and energy responsible for our vast education system; the abolition of slavery; the settlement of refugees; the creation of our national park system; the galaxy of different local religious congregations; the public libraries; women's suffrage; clean water; public social services; historical societies; the vast cultural networks of museums, orchestras, and dance companies; prevention of contagious disease; humane care of the mentally ill; social security; child labor laws; employment of people with disabilities; fire and other emergency services; and on and on.

For almost all of us and our parents and grandparents, too, our lives have been shaped substantially by voluntary institutions, beginning with religion, including religious-related schools and hospitals, the local Y, visiting nurses, scout camp, college, community chest, volunteer fire company, community improvement societies, homes for the aged, and finally, the cemetery.

The great private foundations too—like Rockefeller and Carnegie—were influential in providing the dollars and roadmaps for our pioneering work in everything from education and health to agrarian reform and international understanding.

Many of us remember those earlier days fondly and worry about what's happened to all that neighborliness and charity. There is a generally accepted notion that people don't help out the way they used to. Actually, the truer picture and the good news is that today a greater proportion of our population is involved in volunteering and giving than was true at any time in our history.

It's important to our orientation and morale, and it's important to the volunteers who look to board members for leadership, to know that America's voluntary spirit is alive and well.

Volunteers today achieve a stunning impact on an almost endless number of problems and dreams. The composite of all their individual acts of kindness and courage moves mountains of pain, hopelessness, neglect, and indifference, and with each success, provides hope and examples for all the rest of us.

I don't want to take the slightest chance that these glorious truths about the good that volunteers do will be lost or diluted in abstract praise, so let me be very precise about the current impact.

- In just the past twenty years, volunteers have broken through centuries of indifference to the needs of the dying, and as a result of their noble crusade, almost every community already has hospice services to provide relief to the terminally ill and their families.

- In very recent times, volunteers' passion, courage, and tenacity have forced the nation and every region in it to realize that we must preserve for future generations our precious resources of water, air, and land. That ethic and practice have now spread to every form of local and national asset including wetlands, forests, farmland, and historic buildings and districts.

- Volunteers stood up and were counted for common decency and adequate services for retarded children, and with those breakthroughs showed the way to many others who then dared to do the same for cerebral palsy, autism, learning disabilities, and hundreds of other problems we hadn't even heard of twenty years ago.

- With the growth of Alcoholics Anonymous, volunteers pioneered a model of mutual assistance that today extends to almost every serious personal problem. In almost every community there's a group of people who have weathered the storm and are reaching out to others newly faced with such threatening crises as the death of a child, mastectomy, depression, stroke, or physical abuse.

- Volunteers sang "we are not afraid"—though of course they were—but with each new volunteer recruited to the crusade, their courage, confidence, and power grew, and then when their vast army sang and believed "we shall overcome," they did.

- The Civil Rights Movement then spread to every disenfranchised and under represented group including women, physically disabled, Native Americans, Hispanics, and so many more.

- A few volunteers, at first mostly parents and students, believed they could do something about drunk driving, but despite the escalating ravages, most of us didn't think they would succeed. Thank God they did.

- With the increasing evidence of the power of ordinary people, more individuals realized that maybe—just maybe—they could also change public policies and behavior about smoking, and look what they've done.

- Dealing with community problems was one thing, but some issues defied organization or were even off-limits for reasons of national security. However, some people believed that matters such as control of nuclear power were linked to survival, so volunteers stepped in, at their peril, to reduce our peril.

- Volunteers even began to take peace into their territory with people-to-people understanding as a fundamental step to reduce international tensions and build tolerance and friendship.

- And all the time a healthy number of people served all of us by promoting the importance and availability of arts and cultural opportunities as central aspects of a civilized society. One of the great waves of voluntary activity and impact has involved community theater, dance, and music to provide opportunities for creativity and enjoyment of it.

The list goes on almost endlessly with preschool education, day care, social services, cancer control, consumerism, population control, conflict resolution, ethnic museums, early infant care, independent living for the elderly, teen pregnancy, AIDS, substance abuse, job training, and so very much more. The services and impact of volunteers and voluntary organizations extend from neighborhoods to the ozone layer and beyond. Whether one's interest is wildflowers or civil rights, arthritis or clean air, oriental art or literacy, the dying or the unborn, organizations are already at work, and if they don't suit our passion, it is still a special part of America that we can go out and start our own.

Beyond all the indications of the good that results when so many people do so many good things, it is also important to recognize what all these efforts mean to the kind of people we are. I submit that all this voluntary participation strengthens us as a nation, strengthens our communities, and strengthens and fulfills us as individual human beings.

The Pulitzer Prize-winning historian Merle Curti says, "Emphasis on voluntary initiative has helped give America her national character."

In *How to Succeed with Volunteers*, David Church makes the case that the health of a society can be equated with the degree of citizen involvement. He quotes Professor Marshall E. Dimock of New York University: "When voluntarism is vigorous, the country is vigorous. When it shows signs of decline, we are in trouble."

In preparation for the book *America's Voluntary Spirit*, I examined most of the great citizen crusades in our history. What comes through again and again is that the participation, the caring, and the evidence that people can make a difference add wonderfully to the spirit of our society. In Inez Haynes Irwin's "The Last Days of the Fight for Women's Suffrage" (in *The Story of Alice Paul and the National Woman's Party*), again and again she comes back to the spirit of those women, not only in deciding on the task and accomplishing it, but also what their success meant to them as human beings. She says, for example, that "they developed a sense of comradeship for each other which was half love, half admiration and all reverence. In summing up a fellow worker, they speak first of her 'spirit,' and her spirit is always beautiful, or noble, or glorious."

She describes a moment in 1917 when a group of women, just arrested for picketing at the White House, are shoved into a prison room and, because the experience is so foreign, they are terrified by the immediate and the long-term consequences of their arrests. At the far end of the room is the wave of women who were arrested the day before—but no verbal communication is allowed between the two contingents. In a gesture to calm, encourage, and salute, the veterans "raised their water glasses high, then lowered them and drank to their comrades."

That spirit comes through in each of the great reform movements. It becomes clear that when people make the effort, not only are causes and people helped, but also something special happens for the giver too, and the community and the nation take on a spirit that is so much a part of our national character.

It is interesting and instructive to realize that when one thinks of the giants of the independent sector, one is as likely to think of women's names—at least in the last 150 years—such as Clara Barton, Jane Addams, Mary McLeod Bethune, Susan B. Anthony, Dorothea Dix, Alice Paul, Elizabeth Cady Stanton, Harriet Beecher Stowe, Dorothy Day, Mother Seton, Carrie Nation, Margaret Sanger, Lucretia Mott, Mary Lasker, and on and on. The voluntary sector is the only one of our three sectors that at least has begun to tap the full spectrum of the nation's talent.

It's easy for the individual to think that she or he can't make much of a difference, but in a democracy that encourages diversity, innovation, and criticism, it is often an individual or small group that starts a cause and even a crusade. It has become almost trite to quote Edward Everett Hale's motto for the Lend a Hand Society, but it still captures the importance of each person making an effort:

> I am only one,
> But still I am one,
> I cannot do everything,
> But still I can do something;
> And because I cannot do everything
> I will not refuse to do the something
> that I can do.

Not long ago, I was fascinated to come across an essay from *McGuffey's Reader* written in 1844. It is entitled "True and False Philanthropy" and offers one of the most succinct lessons about why people must care about their neighbors and others.

The essay starts with Mr. Fantom talking about global designs for doing good, while Mr. Goodman is trying to get him to focus on needs closer to home. Mr. Fantom says, "I despise a narrow field. Oh, for the reign of universal benevolence! I want to make all mankind good and happy." Mr. Goodman responds, "Dear me! Sure that must be a wholesome sort of a job: Had you not better try your hand at a *town* or *neighborhood* first?"

With disdain Mr. Fantom retorts, "Sir, I have a plan in my head for relieving the miseries of the whole world. Everything is bad as it now stands. I would alter all the laws, and put an end to all the wars of the world. *This* is what I call doing things on a grand scale."

Mr. Goodman brings up a great many local needs, and Mr. Fantom disparages the attention that each would take away from global solutions. Finally Mr. Fantom says, "I despise the man whose benevolence is swallowed up in the narrow concerns of his own family, or village, or country." The lesson ends with this exchange:

> **Mr. Goodman:** "But one must begin to love somewhere; and I think it is as natural to love one's own family, and to do good in one's own neighborhood, as to anybody else, and if every man in every family, village and country did the same, why then all the schemes would be met, and the end of one village or town where I was doing good, would be the beginning of another village where somebody else was doing good; so my schemes would jut into my neighbor's; his projects would unite with those of some other local reformer; and all would fit with a sort of dovetail exactness."
>
> **Mr. Fantom snorts:** "Sir, a man of large views will be on the watch for great occasions to prove his benevolence."
>
> **Mr. Goodman concludes:** "Yes, sir; but if they are so distant that he cannot reach them, or so vast that he cannot grasp them, he may let a thousand little, snug, kind, good actions slip through his fingers in the meantime; and so, between the great things that he *cannot* do, and the little ones that he *will not* do, life passes, and *nothing* will be done."

When one out of every two Americans regularly helps to improve our shared condition, the country as a whole takes on a spirit of compassion, comradeship, and confidence. In the most fundamental ways, 100 million volunteers make America a participatory and successful nation.

3

Today's Volunteers: Who Volunteers and for What Causes?

At times just about every volunteer reaches the point of wondering, "Why me? or even, "Why does it always have to be me? And occasionally, "Why me, Oh Lord, why me?"

Sometimes we seem to be the only ones ever asked to volunteer—and at that point we damn the askers. Sometimes we seem to be the only ones who say yes—and at that point we damn ourselves and wonder if we should have our heads examined.

It may be helpful to your sanity—and to your spirit—to know that recent surveys indicate that approximately half of American adults are regular volunteers, and nearly seven out of ten volunteers report that they participate on a regular basis, monthly or more often.

The base of participation is also widening. More young people, more men, and more older people are volunteering. Every economic and ethnic group is involved. To the surprise of all who have matter-of-factly assumed that with so many women now in the workforce, it's harder to find female volunteers, the happy reality is that women who work for pay are more likely to volunteer than women who don't.

Some other figures are also encouraging:

- The 40–49 age group is the most active, with almost 50% serving as volunteers; but the other age groups are not far behind: 21–29 years (35%), 30–39 years (48%), 50–64 years (45%), and 65 and over (40%).

- The volunteer ranks include 46 percent of all women and 42 percent of all men.

- Married people are more likely to volunteer (50%), compared to 35% for single people, 37% for widowed, 38% for divorced, 34% for separated, and 31% for those living with a partner.

From another angle, the volunteers surveyed said that these are the reasons they are involved.

• Compassion toward people in need	96.3%
• Giving back to the community	91.0%
• Those who have more should help those with less	90.4%
• Volunteering is an important activity to people one respects	83.2%
• Someone close is involved in the activity or would benefit from it	68.7%
• Meeting new people	66.4%

And, a number of patterns have surfaced regarding the motivations for volunteering:

- People are much more likely to volunteer or give when asked. Sixty-three percent of people said "yes" when asked to volunteer, whereas only 25 percent volunteer without being asked. And 95 percent of households contribute when asked, compared to 79 percent of the non-asked group.

- People who volunteered as young people are much more likely to maintain that involvement as adults.

The obvious question is for what groups and causes do these people volunteer? Drawing from the INDEPENDENT SECTOR giving and volunteering surveys, the general categories are these:

- Religious organizations   28.4%
- Youth development   15.7%
- Education   12.6%
- Health   9.2%
- Human services   9.1%
- Public or societal benefit   5.1%
- Environment, including animal welfare   4.2%
- Arts, culture, and humanities   2.9%
- Private and community foundations   2.5%
- Adult recreation   1.9%
- Political organizations and campaigns   1.2%
- Work-related   0.9%
- International or foreign programs   0.4%
- Other   5.9%

There have been several important changes in patterns of volunteering. People are more likely to spread their volunteering over several different causes. They are also likely to be interested in advocacy and activism. While people are still very much involved in providing services, they also want to make a difference through petitions, studies, testimony, and other forms of active citizen participation. Another difference involves the women who work for pay. Although they are still active as volunteers, they rarely can give that full day or several evenings a week to the church or hospital.

With these changes in the patterns of volunteering, the situation facing the volunteer recruiter is either very bad news or very good news. For the organization that is still trying to get large amounts of time from a relatively few middle- and upper-income women in the immediate neighborhood, the picture is discouraging. For the recruiter willing to include a broader spectrum of geography, gender, age, ethnicity, and economic group, and willing to break the assignments down into more reasonable size, the news is very good. In addition, this broader outreach can spread news of the institution and its program activities and can increase its influence and impact.

It is important to add one more thought on the matter of advocacy and service. For a while, some of the women's organizations saw volunteering as demeaning to women. They characterized volunteers and voluntary organizations as "do gooderism" in the most negative sense. I always point out that the women's movement and activist women's organizations are among the most encouraging examples of voluntary initiative, adding that the most significant contribution of volunteers and voluntary organizations has been in the great crusades involving human rights. However, if some people choose also to be involved in direct service to help others, this, too, is an important way to make a difference. It helps causes and people, humanizes an organization's approach to its job, and provides a degree of citizen education that often leads to the most effective advocacy.

One aspect of personal service relates to the burgeoning growth of what we call the self-help movement, but for which the British have the much better term, mutual aid. The mutual help movement is the fastest growing side of the voluntary sector. For almost every problem, there is now a group of people who have weathered the storm and are reaching out to help others newly faced with loss of a child, depression, alcoholism, divorce, physical abuse, heart surgery, or almost any imaginable vulnerability.

Some people look at all these advocacy and mutual help activities and suggest that this is not volunteering, "at least in the old or real sense." I often hear people say that volunteering should describe only the act of helping others less fortunate. These same people almost always use the barn-raising as their quintessential example. I believe as passionately as they that one of the best motivations and forms of volunteering is embodied in the religious teachings involving charity to others. But we can't ascribe our tradition of voluntary action solely to these lessons and examples of goodness. The matter of pure need and mutual assistance cannot be overlooked. The Minutemen and the frontier families who built one another's barns practiced pretty basic forms of enlightened self-interest. To portray our history of volunteering as relating solely to goodness may describe the best of our forebears, but it ignores the widespread tradition of organized neighborliness that hardship dictated and goodness tempered.

The important thing is that more people are involved in all kinds of causes today and have more opportunities to influence their lives and to be of service to others. Happily, we have moved by stages from the exclusive level of Lord and Lady Bountiful, through the period of the elite "400" and the years of the concentrated power structure, and are now beginning to recognize that participatory democracy is everybody's business. We owe a debt of gratitude to Dorothea Dix and her kind of crusaders and to the community fathers who served so many causes; but the grandest huzzahs should be reserved for the here and now, when democracy has truly come alive, with all parts of the population joining in the traditions of service and reform. Today, anyone who cares and who is prepared to do something can make a difference.

We usher, collect, inform, protest, assist, teach, heal, contribute, build, advocate, comfort, testify, support, solicit, canvas, demonstrate, guide, criticize, organize, appeal, and—in a hundred other ways—serve people and causes.

Many people don't understand how much volunteering means to our society, or even have a grasp of the dimensions of it, because this is an aspect of our national life that we take for granted and have never really felt a need to study. Now that there seems to be a growing realization that citizen participation is a vital part of our national character, there is a greater interest in having a clearer grasp of the facts, trends, and impact.

Misunderstanding exists on the giving side also. Most people assume that foundations and corporations represent the largest proportion of giving in America. As important as their dollars are, the two groups combined represent only 15 percent of all that is given. Eighty-five percent comes from individuals, including their bequests.

Also, contributors with incomes under $25,000 give proportionately more of their income than do contributors with incomes of $100,000.

The 2001 INDEPENDENT SECTOR survey conducted by Gallup pointed out that approximately 89 percent of all American adults make contributions to the causes of their choice.

According to *Giving USA.*, published by the American Association of Fund-raising Counsel's Trust for Philanthropy, these are the general areas to which we give our contributions:

- Religion   36.7%
- Education   15.0%
- Health and hospitals   8.9%
- Human services   8.5%
- Arts and culture   5.5%
- Civic and public   5.5%
- Environment   2.9%
- International   1.7%
- Other   15.2%

These general causes or categories are represented by at least one million specific voluntary organizations to which we give our time and money. Were there an accurate count of churches or of local units of national organizations, or of the thousands of organizations that do not have to apply for tax-exempt status, we would be dealing with several million organizations in the independent sector.

John W. Gardner noted that:

The sector encompasses a remarkable array of American institutions— libraries, museums, religious organizations, schools and colleges, organizations concerned with health and welfare, citizen action groups, neighborhood organizations and countless other groups such as Alcoholics Anonymous, the Urban League, the 4-H Clubs, Women's Political Caucus, Salvation Army and United Way.

Americans have always believed in pluralism—the idea that a free nation should be hospitable to many sources of initiative, many kinds of institutions, many conflicting beliefs, and many competing economic units. Our pluralism allows individuals and groups to pursue goals that they themselves formulate, and out of that pluralism has come virtually all of our creativity.

Beyond the urgent causes and crusades, the independent sector simply provides people with a chance to do their own thing—to be different, to be free, to be unique. In an Occasional Paper, "The Third Sector: Keystone of a Caring Society," published by INDEPENDENT SECTOR, Waldemar Nielsen, drawing in part from his book, *The Endangered Sector,* summarized the variety of interests that Americans freely pursue through their voluntary organizations, for example:

If your interest is people, you can help the elderly by a contribution to the Grey Panthers; or teenagers through the Jean Teen Scene of Chicago; or young children through your local nursery school; or everyone by giving to the Rock of All Ages in Philadelphia.

If your interest is animals, there is the ASPCA and Adopt-A-Pet; if fishes, the Isaac Walton League; if birds, the American Homing Pigeon Institute or the Easter Bird Banding Association.

If you are a WASP, there is the English Speaking Union and the Mayflower Descendants Association; if you have a still older association with the country, there is the Redcliff Chippewa Fund or the Museum of the American Indian.

If your vision is local, there is the Cook County Special Bail Project and Clean Up the Ghetto in Philadelphia; if national, there is America the Beautiful; if global, there is the United Nations Association; if celestial, there are the Sidewalk Astronomers of San Francisco.

If you are interested in tradition and social continuity, there is the society for the Preservation of Historic Landmarks and the Portland Friends of Cast Iron Architecture; if social change is your passion, there is Common Cause; and if that seems too sober for you, there is the Union of Radical Political Revolutionary Satire in New York.

If your pleasure is music, there is a supermarket of choices—from Vocal Jazz to the Philharmonic Society to the American Guild of English Hand Bellringers.

If you don't know quite what you want, there is Get Your Head Together, Inc. of Glen Ridge, New Jersey. If your interests are contradictory, there is the Great Silence Broadcasting Foundation of California. If they are ambiguous, there is the Tombstone Health Service of Arizona.

John W. Gardner added, "If you can't find a nonprofit institution that you can honestly disrespect, then something has gone wrong with our pluralism."

All this voluntary effort and the giving that supports it enable us to be unique as individuals and as a society. Through our voluntary initiative and independent institutions, ever more Americans worship freely, study quietly, are cared for compassionately, experiment creatively, serve effectively, advocate aggressively, and contribute generously. These national traits are constantly beautiful and, we hope, will remain beautifully constant.

PART II

Making a Difference:
The Role of the Board

4

The Role of the Board and Board Members

An interesting list of objectives for the ideal board member, attributed to Michael Davis of the Rosenwald Fund, has endured for more than fifty years. Here are five of his best:

- Know why the organization exists, and annually review why it should.

- Give money, or help get it, or both.

- Face budgets with courage, endowments with doubt, deficits with dismay, and recover quickly from the surplus.

- Interpret the organization's work to the public in words of two syllables.

- Combine a New England sense of obligation with an Irish sense of humor.

Boards of directors differ according to the organization's size and age, if it functions as a federation or a single institution, if it has a staff, and whether it is a service organization with the board having ultimate authority, or a cause-oriented association where the membership body shares responsibility.

There are some universal truths applicable to every nonprofit organization, beginning with legal responsibility. Whether as board members you are called trustees, directors, governors, or something else, you are in essence the trustees in the literal and legal sense of the term. No matter how the organization is structured or the degree of authority delegated to staff, committees, or affiliates, the board and therefore the trustees are ultimately accountable.

In the 1984 court action in New Jersey involving an organization called Friends of Clinton Hill, a sympathetic judge listened to the board members' reasons for not knowing that their association had failed to pay the government for income taxes withheld or for social security taxes. He described these volunteers with such terms as *selfless, dedicated*, and *compassionate* but said nevertheless that the law left him no alternative but to hold them accountable for all such taxes and stiff interest penalties.

Whether it is a service agency or a cause-oriented membership association, the board has the principal responsibility for fulfillment of the organization's mission and the legal accountability for its operations. Usually the bylaws stipulate something like, "The affairs of the corporation are vested with the board." There have been several legal cases where board members were held legally accountable, largely because they had failed to exercise reasonable oversight and objectivity. When those cases are reported in the newspapers, the trustees are often quoted as, ". . . not having seen financial reports," ". . . not having known," or ". . . not aware that the organization had contracted with a firm owned by one of the staff or board members," or in other ways making clear that the trustees had not taken responsibility for knowing what was going on.

The law, however, is fair as long as a trustee's attention to responsibility is reasonable. Joseph Weber, former head of the Greater New York Fund, pointed out in "Managing the Board of Directors" that, ". . . this does not mean that a director needs to fear liability for every corporate loss or mishap that may occur. On the contrary, a Director is generally protected from liability for errors of judgment as long as he or she acts responsibly and in good faith, and with the basic interests of the corporation as the foremost objective."

Although the legal responsibility is real, and some boards and agencies are highly complex, the role of the board should still be seen in the fairly simple framework of "What are trustees accountable for?"

The BBB Wise Giving Alliance (a merger of the Better Business Bureau's Philanthropic Advisory Service and the National Charities Information Bureau) has developed "Standards for Charitable Accountability" and indicates that, "Organizations that comply with these accountability standards have provided documentation that they meet basic standards . . . in how they govern their organization, in the ways they spend their money, in the truthfulness of their representations, and in their willingness to disclose basic information to the public."

The Alliance Standards also are specific about board performance, for example:

Governance and Oversight

The governing board has the ultimate oversight authority for any charitable organization. This section of the standards seeks to ensure that the volunteer board is active, independent and free of self-dealing. To meet these standards, the organization shall have:

1. **A board of directors that provides adequate oversight of the charity's operations and its staff.** Indication of adequate oversight includes, but is not limited to, regularly scheduled appraisals of the CEO's performance, evidence of disbursement controls such as board approval of the budget, fund raising practices, establishment of a conflict of interest policy and establishment of accounting procedures sufficient to safeguard charity finances.

2. **A board of directors with a minimum of five voting members.**

3. **A minimum of three evenly spaced meetings per year of the full governing body with a majority in attendance, with face-to-face participation.** A conference call of the full board can substitute for one of the three meetings of the governing body. For all meetings, alternative modes of participation are acceptable for those with physical disabilities.

4. Not more than one or 10% (whichever is greater) directly or indirectly compensated persons(s) serving as voting member(s) of the board. Compensated members shall not serve as the board's chair or treasurer.

5. No transaction(s) in which any board or staff members have *material* conflicting interests with the charity resulting from any relationship or business affiliation. Factors that will be considered when concluding whether or not a related party transaction constitutes a conflict of interest and if such a conflict is material, include, but are not limited to: any arm's length procedures established by the charity; the size of the transaction relative to like expenses of the charity; whether the interested party participated in the board vote on the transaction; if competitive bids were sought and whether the transaction is one-time, recurring or ongoing.

Other of the Alliance Standards appear in parts of this book, relating to such relevant topics as evaluations, finances, and fundraising. For your easy reference the complete standards appear in Appendix B and the full current standards are available from the BBB Wise Giving Alliance, 4200 Wilson Boulevard, Suite 800, Arlington, VA 22203, tel. 703-276-0100 or on the www.give.org web site.

Marc Owens, an Alliance board member and former director of the IRS Exempt Organizations Division from 1990–2000, confirmed the comprehensiveness of the new standards. "Over the years, I have seen quite a broad range of problems regarding the accountability of charitable organizations. These proposed new charity standards comprehensively address both existing and emerging ethical issues facing charities today."

It's revealing that the Standards emphasize the role of the board itself. Although it may seem simplistic to say that the first role of the board is to be sure that the board is fulfilling its role, that's often the last place where accountability is exercised. Board members blame staff, committees, the fundraising chairman, the treasurer, and everyone else for failures in the operation, but rarely take a look at whether the board itself meets the kind of standards laid down for boards by the Alliance.

In "Major Challenges to Philanthropy," a paper commissioned by INDE-PENDENT SECTOR, Robert L. Payton, former president of the Exxon Education Foundation and later director of Indiana University's Center on Philanthropy, put it on the line:

> As a group, it is the trustees who are most important in protecting the standards of philanthropy. If you smile at that, knowing from our own experience of trustees whose ignorance or single-mindedness made them part of the problem rather than part of the solution, I also smile—but in pained discomfort. Like it or not, the trustees are the structural bulwark defending the public interest in philanthropy. And if I'm right about that, then the education of trustees claims a very high priority on our collective agenda.

Kenneth N. Dayton, former chief executive officer of Dayton Hudson, has served on many corporate, foundation, and large and small voluntary agency boards and has this to say about the similarities and differences in the boards' responsibilities:

> It is my experience that a board's role in the governance of nonprofit organizations—both philanthropic and voluntary—is exactly the same as it is in for-profit corporations.

> This covers moral and legal responsibility, strategy determination, allocation of resources, goal setting, evaluation of performance, rewarding and motivating management, making the tough decisions on top personnel, and being willing and available to assist in the areas of special experience. (It also involves strengthening the board itself—determining criteria for membership and setting policies for tenure and rotation.)

> Those board roles are absolutely essential to the effectiveness of all Public corporations—profit and nonprofit. Contrary to popular notion, I've found that it is often on the nonprofit side that boards take those responsibilities most seriously.

Dayton's last point about the degree of responsibility exercised by volunteer trustees contradicts other perceptions, but if one thinks about it, although the businessperson serving as an outside director of a corporation might take that responsibility seriously in terms of prestige, attendance, and legal liability, he or she really knows that the trustee's role means far more to the success of the institution in the voluntary world. A business corporation obviously needs its board for legal and practical reasons, but it isn't nearly so dependent on those *individuals* for its income and community outreach. Nor is it likely that corporate board members serve on the sales, marketing, and manufacturing committees as they do on the nonprofit organization's rehabilitation, fundraising, and public relations committees.

Because volunteers are necessarily and appropriately involved in many of the day-to-day activities of the organization, including fundraising, annual meetings, program projects, and much more, it's understandable that at the board table there is confusion when people are functioning as trustees and when they are wearing their more general volunteer hats.

It's absolutely essential that the directors function quite literally as the trustees on matters of budgets, audits, evaluations, formal plans, hiring the executive director and assessing performance, but these governance functions are usually only a relatively small part of a board meeting. Much of the time they are not sitting as trustees but rather sitting as interested volunteers helping think through public relations strategies, building annual meeting attendance, or assessing the effectiveness of a special event.

In these matters, the boards, out of enthusiasm and concern, tend to function as extensions of committees and staff, but because they are at the board table, trustees tend to make motions and decisions that seriously confuse who does what in the organization. It's inevitable that interested volunteer board members will become involved in such discussions. To try to make clear when the trustees are functioning in a governance role and when they are functioning as informed, but still informal, advisers to committees and staff, board agendas should be divided into governance matters that require trustee discussion and action and other matters on which the board might wish to provide opinions or be informed.

I've always been fascinated by how quickly serious problems within boards are dissipated when the distinction becomes clear between the trustee role of board members and their other volunteer functions.

Many boards also tend to become confused and even divided when board members feel that they are champions of various parts of the organization, such as the research or library function, and woe to anybody who challenges that particular aspect of the association's work. It's natural that board members might have a special interest in and even some responsibility for parts of the organization, but it's essential that they be reminded of and function in their role as trustees responsible for the overall health of the organization.

I consulted with one of the largest voluntary organizations in the country and found their board operating almost as a collection of armed camps with almost no one worrying about the good of the organization as a whole. Part of the solution was to add some at-large board members whose charge is to make certain that all directors are constantly reminded of their larger responsibility.

Perhaps even more important is the degree to which voluntary organizations look to individual trustees for leadership. Beyond all the essential procedures and participation to assure accountability, the board of the nonprofit organization has a substantial but rarely defined responsibility and opportunity for leadership.

The National Charities Information Bureau had an extensive checklist under the heading "What a Good Board Member Does"; it's significant that the first point was "inspires and leads."

Usually when we think of leaders and leadership, we envision the towering giant who can do anything or the charismatic magician who can get the rest of us to do anything. In "A Guide For New Trustees," from the Association of Governing Boards, Nancy Axelrod quoted a *Wall Street Journal* article that described the ideal board member as, ". . . a man or woman with the versatility of Leonardo da Vinci, the financial acumen of Bernard Baruch, and the scholarly bent of Erasmus."

Most leadership actually comes from ordinary people who have it in them to rise to responsibility. These people are all around us, leading thousands of community and national institutions through conviction, hard work, and quiet ability to help individuals and organizations see their own roles and worth.

In all of the resource materials I've been reviewing, most of the experts enumerate the kinds of professional experience an organization will need on the board and pay no attention to personal qualities. But when I look at what makes a board tick, it's often the ability to work together that counts, and this depends on qualities that lend themselves to teamwork. In *Governing Boards*, Cyril O. Houle says, "Organization is merely the way by which people relate themselves to one another so as to achieve their common purposes."

In *The Volunteer Board Member In Philanthropy*, the National Charities Information Bureau (now part of the Alliance) listed these qualities of good board members:

1. are dedicated to helping others and modest in the light of their responsibilities as board members.

2. approach their responsibilities in the spirit of a trustee on behalf of contributors, their intended beneficiaries, and the public at large.

3. stand up for their convictions, even at the cost of misunderstanding or disapproval in business or social life.

4. back up other board members and staff, rising to their defense when they are unjustly criticized or attacked.

5. treat staff as a partner in a high calling, maintaining overall supervision and control but not interfering with day-to-day administration.

6. avoid being overawed by others on the board, whether they be executive staff; tycoons of business, labor or society; professionals in social work, education, medicine, etc.

7. welcome information and the best available advice, but reserve the right to arrive at decisions on the basis of their own judgment.

8. respect the right of other board members and of staff to disagree with them and to have a fair hearing of their points of view.

9. accept as routine that decisions must be made by majority vote and will at times go against one or more members.

10. criticize, when necessary, in a constructive way, if possible suggesting an alternative course.

11. recognize that time and energy are limited and that over- commitment may prove self-defeating.

12. endeavor to keep disagreements and controversies impersonal and to promote unity.

13. maintain loyalty to their agency, within a higher loyalty to the welfare of the community and humanity as a whole.

Another important source of guidelines for boards and trustees is *Resource: The BoardSource Catalog,* published regularly by BoardSource (the former National Center for Nonprofit Boards).

I've been through enough board orientation and training sessions to know that many newer board members are frustrated, even exasperated, and want to shout, "But you still haven't told me what I'm supposed to do!"

On the most basic level, you as a board member should understand the mission of the organization, attend board meetings, serve actively on at least one committee, be certain that you and the board as a whole are in control of planning and evaluation, contribute to a sense of camaraderie and teamwork, and ask questions.

At least half of those board members who wanted me to say exactly what they should do are now exclaiming, "That doesn't seem enough!" If it's any help, I can pretty much guarantee that if you'll do those things, the rest will become obvious.

Most lists of fundamentals refer to the trustee's role in raising money. The veteran fundraiser Harold Seymour used to put it bluntly: "Contribute wealth, wisdom and work." Today, in our efforts to be more representative, it's not fair to put the arm on everybody for $10,000, or even $500. On the other hand, I think it is fair to ask all board members, within their means and spheres of contacts, to contribute as much as they can and to help raise money. Asking for this help should be the responsibility of volunteers and not the staff, and no board member should feel above these obligations.

Just a word on another basic responsibility, involving the importance of asking questions. If you don't understand the financial statements or the budget or the issue being voted on, ask questions. Sometimes these are better asked ahead of time or during the break so that you are not taking up too much time, and you can use these opportunities to get a bit of tutoring in areas where you are not as knowledgeable as others. However, the ultimate and necessary task is to understand what you are voting on. I can guarantee that other trustees will be grateful that someone else admits confusion, which will lead to a broader sense of comfort in asking even more questions. If you are accountable and don't understand it, where does that leave you and the organization?

There is a balance between not being intimidated into inactivity and at the same time not feeling guilty if you don't understand everything. It's important not to be among those who feel they must stand up and be counted on every issue. Those kinds are pains in the neck and usually confuse personal privilege with principle. Pick the areas that really seem important and on which others don't seem to be coming forward. Don't be critical of yourself or others because you or they don't seem to understand or don't have an interest in everything. It's not realistic to expect that all board members will have an interest in or a grasp of all the things the organization is doing. My experience is that voluntary agency boards of any size are rarely composed of individuals who have across-the-board interest or knowledge. I find that if a board is effectively organized, some people participating will have an intense interest in certain topics, and others will have a like interest in other issues and that, in total, the group will provide an effective screen for all the issues and reasonable discussion of them.

Don't be afraid of healthy give and take. Among other things, it builds a sense of family. Board meetings should be viewed as healthy arenas for controversy. If the issues are laid out in advance, well formulated, and clearly presented, and if sufficient time is available for debate, then it is healthy and constructive for all board members to question, debate, and disagree.

One of the faults of nonprofit organizations is that the leaders strive for compromise and for unanimous votes. My experience has been that if you are dealing with real issues, striving too hard for compromise and unity may mean that you are not facing squarely the issues themselves, you don't have the right mix of people, or you've watered down the issues until they're harmless and impotent. It's far healthier to have a split vote as long as the issues are on the table, the debate is fair, and there has been sufficient time for consideration.

Providing for fair and objective consideration is easier said than done. Those in charge of the meeting often have strong feelings about the issues, meetings are usually too short for any real discussion, and there is too little advance dissemination of the facts to prepare people for adequate debate and vote.

If there is significant controversy, the organization must take the time to present the issues before the board so that the matter can be decided without feeling that something has been put over on people. There will always be the temptation to slip a touchy matter through to avoid hurt feelings or ill will, or to let the executive committee handle a matter simply because it is potentially upsetting. Don't tolerate any of it. Be certain that a proper process is available and that this process is objectively and fairly followed to the letter.

It is far better to lose even on critical issues as long as the organization comes out of the battle with greater confidence in the integrity of the process.

It's also better to take additional time for debate and decision on major items than to put them behind you. For instance, on a major issue I always suggest that the matter should come up initially for reaction and discussion without a vote, even though this means postponement. It is more conducive to correct decision-making and to confidence in the system to take extra time for consideration and review. Even on lesser matters, I generally favor having the board consider issues at one board meeting for vote at the next. Committee chairpersons and staff members are almost always dismayed when I recommend this process. Usually they have worked hard on a project, on guidelines, or on a position statement, and they feel it's imperative that the vote be taken as soon as possible. My approach is that if the matter is so important, it's worth being sure that the people know the issues. I also believe that with this course, there is more likely to be followership once the vote is taken.

The posture of the leader should be one of patience, tolerance, and flexibility. I include flexibility because leaders will often have their own biases, and yet they especially must be willing to seek out and hear new facts and different opinions. The more important the issue, the more intense the feelings and debate are apt to be. You will find some people dig in their heels very early and are adamant about a given position. You will also find that people tend to describe the issues as a matter of principle or moral right. Generally, if you look closer, you will find they have confused policies with principles, or rules and regulations with philosophy. It's helpful to delineate the important distinctions among philosophy, principles, policies, procedures, rules, and regulations. It's easier to take something lower in the order too seriously simply by confusing it with a higher value.

Although this will not apply to the majority of readers, it is important to say something about the national board of an association with local chapters. It doesn't matter whether the national operation is organized as a corporate headquarters or the hub of a federation; it will still be the central entity and as such must provide dynamic leadership for the total organization. This includes responsibility for the organization's spirit, direction, thrust, policies, and guidelines.

One basic way to reduce built-in tensions and to keep the national level attuned to local needs is to be sure that the national board of directors is composed overwhelmingly of people who come from the affiliates. Even if your organization operates as a tight national corporation, there can't be correct decision-making and follow-through without local volunteers having a substantial part in making the decisions. On the national level, the organization should be very largely peopled and run by individuals who have current or at least recent experience on the firing line. The local affiliates must feel it's their national association, or, regardless of how dynamic the leadership, there won't be followership.

Even if you achieve the ultimate in representation, don't expect harmony to automatically follow. You will still have to work hard at it. Remember Pogo's discovery: "We have met the enemy and he is us."

The object of all the lessons to minimize friction and create unity is to use the wonderful volunteer energy to fight for the cause and not against one another.

That's a pretty good rule for the role of all boards and board members.

5

The Role of the Chief Volunteer Officer

Many volunteer heads of voluntary organizations confide that they're well into the job before they really understand what it's all about. This is sorry state of affairs, particularly because much of what the volunteer president or chairperson's term will mean is represented by what is accomplished during the first months on the job. The planning, recruiting, orienting, training, and other essential leadership functions have to be accomplished and accomplished early if the operation is to have sensible direction and exciting thrust. It's toward the goal of early preparation that the following urgent suggestions are made.

Mr. or Mme. President, you are the person morally responsible for your public agency. No matter how inadequate you may feel or even if you have people to whom you can delegate, you are the person who is accountable to your fellow citizens for the expenditure of their dollars contributed to help your agency pursue its service to society.

In his BoardSource publication, "The Role of the Board Chairperson," Eugene C. Dorsey, a former chairperson of INDEPENDENT SECTOR, states:

The position of chairperson, even in a small nonprofit organization, is one of prestige and recognition, connoting respect and trust of one's peers. It is one of authority and power, for the chairperson governs the board of directors or trustees, and the board governs the agency. It is one of high responsibility, for the financial and program future of the agency rests very largely in the chairperson's hands: he or she guides policy development, and policy determines the fate of the organization.

One of the biggest problems for voluntary agencies, particularly those large enough to have a staff, is that volunteer presidents do not really perform as presidents, usually because they exaggerate the role of the staff. Because this is such a significant failing of voluntary agencies, and because the effective fulfillment of the role of president makes such a fantastic difference in the thrust of an agency, I have separated my comments concerning the presidential role from discussion of relative roles of staff and volunteers. The next chapter will deal with that topic, but now I want to try as hard as I possibly can to help presidents grasp how important they are.

Even if the organization has a staff, a president should step back and view the job from the perspective of an agency with no staff. It may assist you to understand your presidential identity and responsibility if you imagine, at least at an early stage and perhaps periodically during your term, what the task would be like if you did not have staff backup. In an unstaffed Parent-Teachers Association, for example, the president is responsible for the recruitment, orientation, stimulation, and follow-up of all committee chairpersons, and unless the president functions, the organization doesn't go anywhere.

Look at your own table of organization. You probably won't see staff members on it. Such organization charts usually include the board of directors, executive committee, president, and committee chairpersons, and that's the way you should see your job. You are the president, and you've got to go through the basic steps required of the chief of any operation. You are the person most essential to the agency's performance, and, as such, the basic leadership responsibilities rest with you. These responsibilities include planning, recruiting, motivating, coordinating, and evaluating.

One of the problems of large voluntary operations is that planning becomes a staff responsibility. Thus, the volunteers themselves aren't really deciding where the organization should be going, and as a consequence the volunteers don't feel the vital commitment necessary to fulfill ambitious plans. You, as president, have to bring planning back to the volunteer side. And believe me, this is tough to do. Even the aspirations you have, and indeed may have voiced in your inaugural speech, are easily suffocated in the day-to-day crises and tasks that so easily absorb the time you give. As a result of lack of planning, you, the president, become absorbed with what the organization serves up rather than exercising your real opportunity to accomplish the things you set out to achieve.

To remedy this, I sit down as early as possible with my incoming president, and I urge him or her to decide on the one, two, or—at the most—three things he or she wants most to have accomplished when the term is finished. Most presidents make the mistake of starting out with too many aspirations, hoping that somehow they can achieve all those exciting goals. Unfortunately, they don't really pin down what it will take to accomplish the goals. Then, because of lack of focus or the press of immediate problems, the goals never get identified firmly in the organization's mind and rarely are accomplished. Many presidents look back with regret that they never really got their teeth into some of the things that seemed so important to them at the beginning.

You, as president, should think hard and early about the things you really want to accomplish during your term. If the goals are realistic, then despite all the other responsibilities that hit you, somehow you will reserve a portion of your energy and resources to move ahead on your special projects. But you have to plan. You have to decide now what it is you want your organization to have achieved one or two years from now. You've got to involve the board of directors in a shared commitment to those goals and help the organization accomplish them.

It's important not to seek too much change. An organization can sustain or survive only so much upset. Often a president wants to change too many things, with the result that the upset is destructive. In some cases, total reorganization may be indicated, and this should be frankly reviewed with the board so that a basic decision can be made. If that's not the problem, then choose your areas carefully and concentrate on them. Thus, you won't be creating additional problems of morale, suspicion, or anger that would only stand in the way of accomplishing your goals.

Another aspect of planning involves your own schedule. Be sure that you have cleared your docket to give the job the time and devotion it needs, and be sure that your family and associates are aware of the commitment and what it entails.

Involve the full board in deciding attainable goals and the best methods for achieving them. The basic rule is to involve the group in identifying attainable goals and agreeing to stick to them tenaciously. You'll find that at different stages your people will want to change strategy, expand unrealistically, or even retreat, prematurely. Decide *together* what it is that needs to be done and how to go about it, and then tear into that effort with absolute conviction and resolve.

Keep in mind that you're likely a unique individual and probably a strong one. You have to be careful that your leadership does not dominate. Give others a chance to participate, or they won't feel any ownership in the plan. Keep very much in mind that if it is an important cause, you can't do it alone and you will drive others away if you're too overbearing. Think of your primary role as that of a *builder*, and it includes building the board itself. Don't be the know-it-all head of the class who might impress with his grasp of the facts but doesn't genuinely engage the group in thinking, planning, and doing. I recently served on a board whose leader was a solo whirlwind, who even responded to each idea or suggestion from the rest of us with a standard coolness, "I'll take that under advisement." She will never get any further than her own energy and ideas, while that cause or any worthwhile cause requires the talents of a great many good people.

In his piece on chairpersons, Dorsey indicates that, ". . . a good leader inspires others with confidence in him, while a great leader inspires them with confidence in themselves." One of the most fascinating experiences I ever had with board-building involved a director who was so bright and outspoken that he intimidated other board members, and they didn't want to take any chance of crossing him. On the other hand, Harry was so smart and hard working, that on those grounds, he deserved to be the next chairperson. Knowing what that could mean to the board's morale and cohesiveness, the nominating committee balked until a wise and senior member of the group volunteered to have a candid talk with Harry about the difference between a board member's role and that of board leader. Subsequently he reported that all would be well with Harry in the chair and, despite some misgivings, the nominating committee and board awarded Harry the gavel.

Harry turned out to be one of the very best board heads I've ever seen. The difference, it turns out, was the wise person's interpretation, and Harry's acceptance of it, that the absolutely primary role of the leader is to build the board's sense of mutual responsibility and trust, and that that role required a *very* different approach than that of an independent director who believed he had an obligation to speak his mind on everything.

I learned through that experience that most very experienced and well intentioned people who move from board membership to board chairmanship don't really understand, intellectually and practically, that the fundamental distinction in the board leader's role is to be the *builder* of the board. That may appear obvious, but for me it was a breakthrough solution in working with boards that have almost mysteriously gone sour. The chair—or the executive director—takes his or her perceived leadership responsibilities too seriously without realizing that those talents and time should be applied to building the board's capacity for shared leadership and participation.

One of the frustrations you might face is that it may be important to take some steps backward before you move forward. For instance, you may have been involved in the organization much longer than the others, or at least have a good deal more experience with some of the projects and issues at hand, and you will assume that the group understands and accepts the facts as you see them and is ready to move forward. That's not very likely. The other trustees will probably have to cover some of that same ground for themselves. People have got to feel that they personally have gained a grasp of the facts and have a chance to sift through them before they develop a commitment to the course of action.

Often the president leaves the critical task of recruitment to the staff. This doesn't do the job. You, as president, have to decide who it is you really want to assist you to accomplish the things you want to do, manage the ongoing activities, and deal effectively with the crises that are the day-to-day fare of a vibrant voluntary agency.

Don't take the easy way out by simply letting Sally have a fourth term, even though she hasn't been a very good committee chairperson up to now. Don't just hope that Pete will be better in his second year than he was in his first. And don't let the fear of relationship problems stand in the way of doing what's right. These are things that an effective president of any good operation has to face up to, and unless you're willing to undertake conscientiously the job of recruitment of able people, the organization won't aggressively move forward to fulfill your aspirations or even perform its public mission.

Carefully analyze the jobs to be done, and then spend a lot of time identifying the people qualified for them. This is worth a good deal of your time early on or even in advance of your administration. It will not only save time later but make the difference in how much progress is made.

One mistake organizations make is to recruit automatically as leader the expert on a particular subject without regard to his or her organizing skills. We eagerly recruit people to do organizing jobs that they are incapable of doing. If we want to organize a community program to reduce the incidence of stroke, we tend to seek out the cardiologist most experienced with vascular accidents. If we want to organize an advisory board to a community mental health center, we look for psychiatrists and clinical psychologists. If we want to organize a local chapter of the American Cancer Society, we look for a radiologist. Experience instinctively leads me away from such experts as committee heads and toward people with organizing skills. While experts should be an important part of the committee, they are not likely to have the necessary organizational skills. Also, they may intimidate or otherwise turn off the very group of people whose enthusiasm and activity they should be building.

When setting out to recruit people, the approach is generally characterized by, ". . . get as many as you can—the more the better." The unfortunate result of all this enthusiastic freewheeling is that the recruiters almost always are overly optimistic, and the whole effort tends to crumble when their accomplishments begin to fall short of aspirations. Instead, figure out how many people are needed, and cautiously predict how many of this number can be recruited in the first six months or even the first year. Do it *realistically*. Set *attainable* targets. Divide the workload so that no one person is given an assignment in which failure is almost inevitable. Beware of the individual who wants to impress the group with how much she or he is going to do or how many cards she's going to take or how many friends he's going to sign up. A group that goes at building in a deliberate, realistic way (and this doesn't preclude fervor and determination) will be a lot farther ahead at the end of a year than the group put together by optimists who assume that their enthusiasm will carry the day.

Numbers are important, but so are the right people. Identify who you need on your side to put together the facts or the strategy and who will have the capacity to put that strategy to work. There will be times when you won't want people who already occupy seats in the power structure because they represent the status quo, and that's what you want to change. Do not assume that you can't get somebody and move ahead to form a committee of lesser impact.

Identify the people, or at least the types of people you need, and launch an effort to get the right persons to join you. You will be surprised how often they will say yes or lead you to other good people.

Effective people turn down appointments not because they are uninterested, but because the assignments are put to them in such a vague way that they fear saying yes could lead them into a bottomless pit of responsibility. Often we ask a person to come aboard without making clear exactly why we want him or her and without breaking the task down into reasonable assignments. If you ask a member of the school board to help with a committee looking at special education, ask him or her to sit in on those committee meetings that will include the topic. We make a mistake in assuming that in order to be effective, someone has to join the committee or board, when we are likely to enlist more of the right people by involving them only in the bite-size ad hoc assignments for which they are really needed.

Break the job down into specific assignments so the individuals can grasp exactly what you want and will not be frightened by the implications of the commitment. Let them know you will be around to help. There is nothing worse than coming out of a hard sell only to wake up to find the leader acting as if he or she has got the sucker and is off to other victories. You have a responsibility to assist this individual in doing the very things you have been struggling with in your own assignment, including deciding what's needed, identifying the sources of help, and recruiting people.

The greatest temptation in recruiting volunteers is to make the job sound easy. It's natural to be eager to get a yes, but in the long run this deception will catch up with you. It is better to give the individual a clear picture of the assignment, so that when you get a yes, you will know you've got someone who is committed to getting the job done. It's better to get a few who say no than to end up with someone who isn't likely to produce, or who can't be held accountable because there is no mutual understanding of what is to be done. Keep in mind that you want to come out of your recruiting effort with an individual who knows what is expected and is eagerly looking forward to getting it done.

Recruiting does involve enthusiasm. People have to know by your approach that this is something you believe in and that it merits their time and attention. People want a cause—even busy people are willing to be further involved if they feel their service will make a difference. Don't assume that people already know about the cause. This applies even to persons who have been serving on committees or as board members. When you recruit someone for a key job, take the time to be sure that he or she knows the cause. This is likely to build a more positive frame of reference and a feeling of being part of something worthwhile.

Orientation begins during the recruitment process. This includes orientation to the cause, to the organization, and to the individual's job. Each person needs special attention, and the effectiveness of these efforts will often determine whether or not the individual in fact succeeds. Orientation is often dismissed by giving the poor individual an unbelievable amount of material that won't be read or understood. Think carefully about the people your recruit should meet if he or she is to gain greater knowledge or enthusiasm about the cause, and set up these appointments either on a one-to-one basis or in small groups. Put yourself in the place of the new person, and figure out what he or she really needs to know in order to increase interest and enthusiasm and to fulfill the assignment effectively.

In addition to initial orientation to the cause and the agency, most volunteers should receive continuing orientation so that they will feel abreast of the agency's impact on the cause. Often orientation, if done at all, is limited to the first few weeks; then we assume individuals learn all they need to know from occasional contacts with the organization.

People will stay with your effort if they feel useful—feel that they are doing some good and that the agency represents a cause worth devoting their energy to. These factors, in turn, relate to the leader's responsibility: 1) to give people jobs that are accomplishable, 2) to give them an awareness of the effectiveness of the good work the organization is doing, and 3) to offer every possible opportunity to learn that they are making a difference. Giving people responsibility commensurate with their abilities and levels of interest is also a key to retention. People are just as apt to walk away if they feel they are being underused as if they are being overused.

Most important causes require sustained effort and depend upon a great many volunteers working together in a systematic way. When a good-sized army is needed, a conscious effort must be devoted to building the organization. Many organizations gravely underestimate this, and their voluntary operations are disastrous. Building an organization begins with training the current leaders to recognize the need to devote time and resources toward increasing the capacity of the operation. This may seem easily done, but it's usually not done at all. The leaders are so impatient to be on with the crusade that they assume that everybody feels the same fervor and knows what to do instinctively. An organization's leaders must be shown the necessity of building the organization to match the goals, and they must have help in learning how to do it.

In training sessions for volunteer and staff leaders, I use a two-part presentation entitled "Achievements Worth Building For" and "Building for Greater Achievement." This provides an opportunity to present the accomplishments we can achieve, while at the same time making clear that the achievements will be realized only if we build an effective organization capable of such fulfillment.

Even after presidents have given realistic attention to planning, recruiting, and orientation, they usually leave the rest to staff or to chance. Staff members can carry a good share of the load of volunteer training and development, but your presence must still be felt. Your efforts in effectively involving your key partners in major activities and decision-making are essential. Keep in mind that these are *your* people. Committee heads, project chairpersons, and other officers are *your* partners. They want to know what *you* think, they want to know where *you* are going, they want to know how *you* perceive the organization, and they want to know what *you* consider important to be done.

Most presidents assume that this kind of thing just happens, that the executive has somehow communicated all these things, or that a past chairperson has oriented a successor; or even that a person, simply by having been a member of the board, has a grasp of the new and larger responsibility. There can't be cohesion in the organization without your involvement in orientation and training and without your giving a great deal of thought about how to effectively motivate, inspire, and stimulate persons who will be carrying the major part of the load. The organization can't move as a unified phalanx toward the goals set by you and the board unless your key partners have participated with you in deciding where the organization is going and feel they are really an integral part of the operation.

You also must function as the motivator, encourager, and prodder. You've got to provide regular opportunities for discussion of progress and problems. It's important to be on that phone five or six times during the year just to say, "Mary, how's it going? I heard about your meeting last week. I am sorry I couldn't get there, but I am delighted with what I hear about it. Is there anything I can do? We're putting you on the agenda of the board meeting, and we're really looking forward to that report. I hope we'll get the material well in advance, so everybody can enjoy it and act intelligently on it."

Don't assume that if you're regularly communicating with the executive director, you're really touching base with your own key volunteers. They are human beings, and an organization will respond far better if you, as the leader, are in touch with your principal lieutenants in a human way. If they feel you're really interested, they'll respond; they'll perform similarly with the people responsible to them, and the total operation will be many times stronger. Obviously, it's important not to overlook the need of people to have their backs patted and, in some cases, their performance questioned—and only the president can perform these functions.

It's your responsibility to see that the activities that the officers, board of directors, and committee heads set out to do are being carried out. One of the basic approaches is to have certain checkpoints during the year. At these times, provide project and committee chairpersons with an opportunity to report at meetings of the board of directors. It will also be important for you to stay close enough to be able to judge the progress or lack of it and to sit down with the chairpersons to discuss any impediments.

If a key subordinate is letting you down, face up to the task of replacement. Usually the individual will be relieved to be out from under the responsibility. But even if he or she is unhappy with your action, your larger responsibility is to the contributors and to your community.

To have time for basic management responsibilities, it will be essential for you to avoid being directly responsible for immediate projects. Find people who can carry these projects for you. Your function and goal is to see that the volunteer talent of the organization is being developed. To the extent that you get trapped into assuming responsibility for individual projects and issues, you will not be using your limited time to expand the capacity of the organization to deal with an increasing number of projects and issues.

Be fully conditioned to the human relationship aspects of the role of president. Be prepared and leave time for dealing with many different personalities, most of whom at some point will need soothing, stroking, and encouragement.

Your success will be measured in three important ways: 1) the achievement of the things you set out to accomplish; 2) the fulfillment of the organization's other major projects and its response to unexpected crises and opportunities; and 3) the increase in volunteer involvement, leadership, and responsibility that has been generated during your term.

Develop a checklist to gauge progress on the specific tasks set out at the beginning of the year and to measure increased volunteer activity. At midyear, sit down with some objective persons you can trust and take a hard look at the progress or lack thereof. If you know that you're going to be doing this at various checkpoints, it will increase your determination to come off with good scores.

Over the years I've developed a list of "musts" for presidents. Individual situations vary, and perhaps not all of these will fit your circumstances, but my observation is that the president who rates well on this checklist will be running an exciting operation. On the other side, in the breakdowns I've seen of presidential leadership in nonprofit organizations, the failures can usually be traced to ignoring some of these musts:

- Decide in advance that your largest goal for the year will be to increase the degree of volunteer leadership within the organization.

- Be the president. This leadership role cannot be delegated to the staff, and to the extent that you are confused about your leadership responsibility or that you turn over this role to staff, your success will be compromised.

- Involve your key officers and other colleagues, including staff, in a planning session to determine effectively where you as a team want to be at the end of your term. Be sure that these plans are realistic and attainable. Be sure that the board of directors has the final opportunity to approve them.

- Approve all board of directors and executive committee meeting agendas, and make certain that these are sent out at least ten days in advance of the meetings. Much of what you will be trying to do as the leader of the organization will be lost unless these meetings are your meetings and represent your checkpoints for progress toward the year's goals. It is essential that the agendas be sent in advance so thoughtful people can give thorough consideration to the issues.

- Involve your key partners, and keep in regular personal touch with them.

- Appoint, orient, encourage, and follow up on your project and committee chairpersons. If you leave it to the staff, it may be done, but it won't be accomplished with the same degree of warmth that your personal contact supplies.

- Plan regular meetings with your executive director. Set aside ample time so that the two of you can get into some of the current issues and have enough time left over to check on progress or lack of it on the year's goals.

- Plan for the annual evaluation of the executive director. Even if he or she is tops, small problems can grow into larger ones if there is not some process by which the volunteers can make observations and suggestions. Build it into the system that the board of directors should do the annual evaluation, and then set aside time for it.

- Build positive relationships within the total organization. If your group is part of a larger organization, develop personal relationships with the volunteer leaders at the other levels. Try to do everything possible to minimize friction and to promote effective relationships.

- Make it exciting and worthwhile. Keep in mind your unique position and opportunity to know what's going on in the organization. Provide regular occasions through board meetings, newsletters, personal communications, and every other possible way to help your fellow volunteers enjoy the fun of being part of an organization that is making a difference.

- Realize that you are responsible. If you leave a void, it will be filled of necessity by the executive director, who thereby will become too influential and too preoccupied with doing your job to help expand volunteer involvement and impact. Don't worry about making the staff director too important. The greater danger occurs when you let the staff become too important at the expense of building volunteer responsibility.

This chapter has sought to give you a clear perception of your identity and responsibility as president. If you have staff, your role is still the same but you will have skilled hands to help you fulfill your functions. The next chapter is intended to give you and other board members a fuller grasp of the relative roles of volunteers and staff.

6

Board and Staff:
Who Does What?

In the review of the role of the volunteer president, it was useful to try to see the president's job in the context of an agency without a staff. It might be similarly useful to take a look at a voluntary organization that has come to the point of needing and being able to afford a staff person.

In most of this section, I will speak about the cause-oriented membership association, such as an anti-smoking group, rather than the agency providing direct professional services, such as a library or clinic. However, many of these lessons apply to the organization in which professionals provide one-to-one services. Later in the chapter, I'll come back to some of the distinctions in board/staff roles in the service operations.

I've observed that most organizations go into a temporary downturn when staff is first hired. The pattern is fairly typical. A wonderful group of dedicated volunteers, through their own individual efforts and without staff backup, have scrambled and scratched their way to having a significant program and are now at the point where they need and might be able to afford some staff assistance. They hire a person, and immediately the volunteers relax, turning much of the work over to the staff director. The volunteers assume that the agency will not only carry on the existing activities but will now be able to spurt forward.

In about one year however, or at the most two, the volunteers may begin to view the scene with bewilderment. They find that the agency is doing less than it was before they hired staff and has lost much of its visibility and vitality. Volunteers will tend to conclude that obviously the wrong person was hired because more was being accomplished when the volunteers were doing it by themselves. Before the downturn and the discouragement become irreversible, the group's members may finally realize that they turned over far too much of the job to the staff and retreated to occasional approvals of what the staff did, along with some irregular assistance to the poor bloke who is president, but who has begun feeling less and less responsible for the operation.

The worst illusion ever perpetrated in the nonprofit field is that the board of directors makes policy and the staff carries it out. This is just not so. The board, with the help of staff, make policy, and the board, with the help of staff, carries it out. Unless volunteers are committed and involved in the action phase of the organization, the agency cannot develop and, in fact, should not be characterized as a voluntary organization. Also, it is naïve to assume that the staff doesn't have considerable influence—usually too much—on policy formulation.

The staff exists to help the volunteers do the work of the organization. Staff members should not be expected or allowed to do the job directly. The greatest sinner is often the president, who far too often gives over his or her responsibility to the executive director.

Most presidents and boards are not certain about the appropriate and relative roles of volunteers and staff in a voluntary agency. Whenever I counsel a president or board, I find it useful to bring them back to the exercise of viewing the organization without staff members so that all the volunteer responsibilities and functions can be clearly identified. Only after that's done do I reintroduce the availability of staff, making it clear that the staff is hired to assist the volunteers to do their citizen jobs in fulfillment of the voluntary agency's mission.

There are two extremes in interpreting the staff's role in voluntary organizations. The first identifies the staff person as the expert who acts principally in an advisory capacity to the interested volunteers. This interpretation is typified by the fundraising consultant who is hired by a church or a hospital to show the volunteers how they themselves can raise a stipulated sum of money. The second identifies the staff person as simply the individual who carries out the clerical details of the agency's function. This interpretation is typified by the part-time executive secretary hired by a service club to arrange details of meetings and handle routine correspondence. In vibrant citizen organizations, the correct role rests squarely between these two. The professional staff person is no less an expert in the specialty than the church's fundraising consultant; neither are the staff functions different from the everyday activities of the service club secretary in handling the routine business that volunteers do not have time to process.

The reason most staff people must be experts and detail people at the same time stems from the nature and magnitude of their organization's mission. Because they are probably working with significant community or national problems, even the details of working out a program and launching it require the daily attention of a skilled community organization specialist. On the other hand, the staff member must be a detail person because he or she is dealing with a problem so comprehensive that no one expert could possibly cope with it alone. An intelligent attack requires the concerted action of many different specialists and community representatives who volunteer their time to determine and pursue solutions.

Voluntary organizations are fortunate in being able to bring the thinking of many specialists to bear on the problems; but in doing so, citizen volunteers must be served with facts, with legwork, and with all the other details that go into making volunteer time pay off. To illustrate how this works in daily operation, take the example of a staff person working in the area of rehabilitation for the American Heart Association. Basically, this person must be knowledgeable about the process of rehabilitation. He or she must know what has been and is being done in rehabilitation to control properly the problem at hand. At this point, the job becomes a matter of feeding all necessary facts to the proper individuals so that the right committee is formed and can as quickly and efficiently as possible devise the right programs to meet the principal needs with which it is concerned. In a sense, the organization and the staff person are picking the brains of these volunteer experts, translating their thinking into a program plan that utilizes existing knowledge and services, working with the committee to modify that plan, and helping the committee launch a program in the community.

In every sense the rehabilitation staff person is servicing the committee with the facts, legwork, knowledge of the agency, knowledge of the community, and an ability to translate the intentions of the volunteers into a plan and, in turn, into the kind of program that the thinkers themselves would inaugurate if the agency could ever afford such a full-time team. Having a staff means that the committee can be utilized to its maximum because the volunteers are not continually bogged down with details or lack of information. In an agency where volunteer leaders can give only limited time, the business of processing details would mean indefinite delays if someone was not available to do this for the committee. With staff, the rehabilitation committee, instead of taking two years to develop and effect one program, can actually develop and undertake many programs in the same time. The basic concept of staff assistance is to leave the big people free to think about the big things and then give them sufficient assistance to translate their thoughts into big results.

A few years ago I collaborated with Geri Joseph, then national volunteer president of the Mental Health Association, to put together a summary of what we, as the chief volunteer and staff officers, jointly considered the essential functions of staff. This is the way we framed the job:

- The role of staff in a voluntary agency is simple in concept (though certainly not in execution). Your job is to bring about the maximum *volunteer* dedication, *volunteer* involvement, and *volunteer* satisfaction.

- You must stimulate, educate, and service. Everything you do must be directly related to the single underlying concept of voluntary action—the promotion of citizen interest in and impact on public matters.

- To the extent you become project oriented and lose sight of your basic role of developing the volunteer capacity of your organization, we might just as well declare ourselves a branch of government. Your mission, your project, your goals, and your record must be measured in increased quotients of volunteer commitment and volunteer results.

We then listed twelve functions staff can perform to make volunteers more responsible and active. These are abbreviated in the following:

- Set one part of your annual goals not in terms of pursuit or completion of specific projects, but in terms of increased volunteer involvement and commitment.

- Provide all possible assistance to help volunteers understand the problems in the field and the role and work of the organization. Volunteers won't feel comfortable and therefore won't give fully of themselves unless they are well informed and briefed on all relevant matters. That doesn't mean sending reams of material; a key part of your job is to summarize information so that it is understandable to volunteers.

- Provide excellent staff service to the president or to the committee chairpersons who rely on you for staff backup. Nowhere is this more critical than in the executive director's responsibility to the president. While the executive director is many things to many people, he or she is also the executive assistant to the president. See that the president has all the information needed to fulfill the obligation as elected head of the organization. Don't do the president's job, but help him or her understand that job and do it well.

- Provide the best possible service to other officers and to the board, committee chairpersons, and committees. If there is one general failing of staff in voluntary organizations, it is that the staff somehow assumes that volunteers are mind readers, that they know the issues and facts. How often we go to committee meetings without the agenda and related details having been distributed in advance. And how often we simply listen to a staff member or an uninformed committee chairperson ramble on about some issue we don't understand, but which must be solved at that very meeting. If you care about the involvement of volunteers—quantity and quality—then be certain that every meeting is carefully preceded by a sharing of the agenda and all pertinent information at least a week in advance. Volunteers can then think about the subject and come prepared to offer competent advice. You'll also find that people will be more willing to come to meetings. If you don't do this, however, many people will feel that the organization is haphazardly run and will not want to be part of hasty decision-making.

- Help identify the points of view and talent needed on the board and on the committees and, to the extent necessary, help in the recruitment of such people. Leave as much of the job as possible to the president and committee chairpersons. Once these people are assembled, let them make the decisions. Don't try to have all the bright ideas. Your skills are needed in knowing the types of people who should be brought together and in giving them the right support. If a staff person or, for that matter, a volunteer assumes that he or she has talents equal to the composite brains and skills of the board or committee, then the organization either has a genius on its hands or, more likely, is in trouble.

- Know the related activities and facilities in your own community. Only to the extent that you really know what is already available can your volunteers help identify gaps, weaknesses, and needs.

- Be certain that your organization operates a competent information and referral program. This may seem a minor point, but the basic service activity of a voluntary agency is to serve as a channel between those who need help and those who can provide it. Often a voluntary agency tends to wait for the glib, exciting projects, when in fact, its fundamental job is to fulfill the basic roles of gadfly, information and referral source, demonstrator, and so on.

- Make planning a priority. Identify those things that most need doing, and then do them well. Despite the many temptations, don't spread yourself so thin that basic obligations and priority projects are not done adequately.

- Stay loose or at least stay flexible. The basic role of a voluntary agency is to see that whatever needs doing is, in fact, accomplished by whomever can do it best. This requires the habit of flexibility— two seemingly contradictory words—and an ability to move from one challenge to another. The role of staff is obviously to be responsive to the need for change.

- Recognize your role as the basic communication link in the organization. Because you represent continuity of service, you are a source of information on the past and about what is happening now in your community and in your organization.

- Keep the dream alive! Don't let yourself be so concerned with the problems you face that you fail to recognize that volunteers look to you to keep the goals in sight. It is up to you to be certain that people are aware of the long-term goals and of the organization's capacity to work effectively toward those goals.

- Provide all possible credit, thanks, and satisfactions for volunteer activity. This will require a good deal of subordination of your own ego, but your goal and your satisfaction must be measured by the degree and quality of volunteer effort achieved.

Of all those points, I'm quite certain that both Geri Joseph and I would give first place to "Keep the dream alive!"

Some of the advice provided so far won't apply equally to the service agency, where most of the work is performed on a one-to-one basis by teachers, therapists, or scientists. However, this is often used as an excuse to keep the board at a comfortable distance. "Raise the money and leave us alone" is sometimes the byword.

Obviously, lay board members should not be substitutes for highly skilled specialists, but neither should the specialization of the program obfuscate the board's role and responsibility, nor should it freeze out the greatest possible utilization of volunteer time and talent.

A few years ago federal budget cutbacks caused significant income reductions for many nonprofit service organizations, and although this caused serious hardship, there were a few healthy lessons. Most of the service organizations whose grants or contracts were cut were determined to preserve as much of their service as possible. Indeed, in the face of growing client needs, they needed to figure out how to do more with less. In the process, many of the most alert and flexible of these organizations rediscovered the volunteer. They relearned how much talent human beings have and how willing people are to be involved in rewarding assignments.

During this period, I saw a great many sensible, sensitive service groups adjust in such remarkable ways as these:

Revitalization of the board. Board revitalization started because the agency desperately needed money. In the process, the organizations learned how much more the trustees could do in financial planning. Many of them had experience in dealing with financial crises. They also brought a practical, common-sense reality to making some hard decisions. Some of the trustees knew how to substitute labor-saving techniques, including automated equipment. Others knew about strategic planning to maximize resources and results. Suddenly it was apparent that these relatively dormant boards had a great deal to offer. In the process of giving they developed a sense of participation and commitment that resulted in far larger fundraising efforts.

Reintroduction of the program volunteer. Even before the recent financial crunch, there was growing criticism of voluntary organizations, including that the staffs were becoming overprofessionalized. In the name of standards and professionalism, many organizations had frozen out the volunteers who had once provided much of the program service. Suddenly, in the face of needing to do more with less and with the help of experienced trustees, these organizations approached it from the other side and began to examine how much of the program could be competently undertaken by less professionally trained individuals. Not surprisingly, they discovered that many of the tasks did not require the certified specialist; they also learned how much ability other individuals have and how much these people can grow with increased responsibility. They began to be more flexible in their hiring practices to involve part-time professionals whose skills were needed. Throughout this process, there was increased reinvolvement of the volunteer through the whole spectrum of program delivery. As stated in earlier chapters, this involvement has benefits far beyond the element of service delivery. These volunteers provide additional sensitivity and caring, they tell the agency's story to hundreds if not thousands of people in the community, and they become loyal advocates.

Greater reliance on consumers and community. In the same spirit of doing more with less, these organizations began looking at other community resources with which they could link for more efficient service. They turned to schools, unions, service clubs, clinics, and other agencies to provide better services at less cost. They also discovered how much the consumers of the services and their families could be involved to extend and improve the services. Just as with the involvement of volunteers, they began to realize how much caring and ability there is in the average human being, how much more the specialist can accomplish by taking time to think about the tasks at hand, and who is available to share the load.

If a service agency wants to remain essentially a voluntary organization, these lessons must be carried over to noncrisis times. Otherwise, if a board is relatively inactive, and if most of the money comes from, and accountability is owed to, government and other third-party sources, then the organization is not really functioning as a voluntary institution.

For the service organization that is not funded by government, these lessons have all the more relevance. To the degree that boards feel needed and responsible, they will contribute enormous talent, outreach, and money.

If the underlying attitude is, "We're just lay board members, what do we know about schizophrenia?" or, conversely, "We're skilled archaeologists, who do the trustees think they are trying to steer our course?"—in either case and from either direction, the impasse will grow, and the organization's characteristics and advantages as a voluntary organization may be lost.

If in the larger society the direction is to help the general public understand the country's options for, say, control of nuclear proliferation or strengthening our public school system, then it should be possible for a group of interested board members to understand your organization's operations, and for all concerned to profit from the composite wisdom and commitment of the total enterprise.

The board will have to be careful not to trespass upon the decisions that require professional judgment, but the number of such decisions should not be exaggerated. When they're necessary, they should be interpreted to the board. Remember that if a *Baltimore Sun* reporter can explain DNA to the public, it is possible for your program specialists to find ways to explain their work to a bright, interested board.

The trustees should not try to decide among treatments A, B, and C, or mathematical theories X, Y, and Z, but they may have to decide whether Program 1 is given priority over Program 2 or whether both are so important that the board will accept a commitment to find funds for each.

Whatever the differences between types of nonprofit organizations, the most important job a board has is to hire the chief staff officer. (Because this is so important, much of Chapter 8 is devoted to it.)

The next most important task is to work with the staff director to be sure that the relative responsibilities of board and staff are understood and fulfilled. For most voluntary organizations, the key issue here is to be sure that the board has the mechanisms by which it can make certain that the staff is not usurping the role of the board—or vice versa. Maintaining this delicate balance is the most difficult part of board/staff relationships and is usually the source of serious breakdowns in agency operations.

Just as it is essential that the board of directors evaluate its own performance, it is equally essential that trustees annually review the executive director's performance. (This, too, is covered in detail in Chapter 8.)

Although the executive director should have absolute authority over other staff members within the organization, the board of directors will exercise ultimate control by its authority to approve the personnel policies and practices of the organization, including the wage and salary administration program. The board also must have firm authority for the basic table of organization—that is, the executive director should not be free to make significant changes in the deployment of staff without the staff organization chart being approved by the board. This is a gray area where staff and board often clash. To me, however, it's an inviolate rule that the board must have authority to pass on the staff structure. Because staff organization and job descriptions carry such influence on future directions and activities, the board must have ultimate responsibility for their determination.

When I began to think about significant reorganization of the American Heart Association staff in Baltimore, I went to the executive committee and outlined the reasons I felt that change was necessary. We had a good deal of discussion as to whether my basic idea had merit, and I was encouraged to develop a more detailed plan. That initial discussion helped clarify and change some of my thinking. I then brought a plan to the executive committee and to the board of directors for their reaction and for discussion. On the basis of those two presentations, I developed a final report that was approved by the executive committee on authority from the board. Once that plan was approved, it was entirely mine to implement with the individuals I chose to recruit, assign, or promote. This was my approach also with two reorganizations of the National Mental Health Association staff.

The board also should be heavily involved in development of one-year and multi-year plans and in the annual evaluation of the fulfillment of those plans.

An area of frequent difficulty in board and executive director relations involves the degree to which the executive director serves as the spokesperson for the agency. In some agencies the executive director serves in this role; in others, the executive director becomes the public spokesperson by default. In still others, the board deliberately wants the executive director to be "Mr. or Ms. Inside," with the public exposure accentuating the volunteer face of the organization. The volunteer leader should generally be the spokesperson. If the topic involves a specialized area, then the volunteer covering that area might speak.

It's important for the organization to have a true volunteer characterization in other ways. It's a good idea to have volunteers representing the organization whenever possible. Staff people should resist almost every opportunity to represent the agency in the community. Often the executive director, because it's the easiest way or because he or she is fascinated by it, will become the association's representative on the community council and on many other advisory boards. An executive director does not belong on any of those committees unless there is some unique factor calling for staff presence. Those responsibilities belong with the volunteers. If they aren't getting this kind of experience, they are not gaining the satisfaction, the encouragement, and the insights they need to become better leaders of the organization.

During the years I was executive director of the National Mental Health Association, I resisted the most tempting invitations to serve on fascinating national boards and committees and to participate in exciting national and international conferences. I turned them down no matter how tempting and no matter how time-consuming it was to find the right volunteer to replace me. Once volunteers are filling these roles, they derive much greater satisfaction from being part of the organization, and their reports are much better received, simply because it isn't always the executive director telling the board about this and that.

Often the staff finds itself so burdened with outside assignments that there is too little time for the basic inside staff jobs. It's essential that the executive director should not become your "Mr. Mental Health Association" or "Ms. Red Cross." This happens so easily and so quickly that it's necessary to be always on guard against it. This is a fair warning for all volunteers, and it is worth repeating: The board should not be too worried about making staff important. The greater danger is in letting staff become too important at the expense of building volunteer responsibility.

The greatest source of friction and breakdown in voluntary organizations of all types, sizes, ages, and relative degrees of sophistication and excellence relates to misunderstandings and differing perceptions between the volunteer president and staff director. I have seen some of the strongest community and national organizations take a sudden tailspin because the individuals, and sometimes the boards, don't agree on the roles of these two leaders.

The problem is seriously exacerbated by the turnover in the chief volunteer officer's position. Whether the tenure is one year, three, or five, new people come with very different understandings of what a chief volunteer officer should be and do. It's also a vulnerable time when a new chief staff officer is hired. The board will assume that the new person has the same grasp of the relative roles and the delicate balance as the predecessor and may be stunned to find a challenge to its cherished authority and prerogatives. In the case of the chief volunteer officer, the board chair may be occupied at one point by the chief executive officer of a very large corporation who overdelegates a large part of his or her responsibility to the chief staff officer, but with new elections that volunteer post may be occupied by a person who has made her reputation through leadership of that city's League of Women Voters, which has no staff, and who therefore is ready to take up the reins—and I mean *all* of them. This may be extreme, but it's not far-fetched. In experience, temperament, and style, each chief volunteer officer is going to be different and in the turnover may meet head-on a chief staff officer who has a pretty fixed notion of his or her own responsibilities, prerogatives, and turf.

A source of this growing problem involves the titles themselves. Increasingly, organizations tend to use the term *chief executive officer* to describe the staff director's position. This can lead to an assumption that the board should be relatively passive, and the chief volunteer officer should stay in the background. If the chief volunteer officer is the chief executive officer, that leads to an impression that he or she is in charge of everything, including the staff director. Because this is where some of the real trouble starts, I think the title of chief executive officer should not apply to nonprofit organizations. Whether the *chief volunteer officer* is called board chairperson or president, the description should be as chief volunteer officer; and whether the staff director is called president, executive vice president, or executive director, the description should be as *chief staff officer*. Voluntary organizations are very different from both business organizations and government agencies, and we only confuse ourselves and our responsibilities by trying to see our roles in contexts that don't altogether apply. Whatever kind of voluntary organization we are dealing with, the role of chief volunteer officer is unique and is not synonymous with those of the chairperson and chief executive of a business corporation.

Similarly, no matter what the size or nature of a voluntary organization, the job of staff president is not the same as the president and chief executive officer of the business corporation. If we try to make the volunteer the chief executive officer, we overstep the bounds of the staff director, and if we try to do the reverse, we assign to the board and its chairperson far too small a role and responsibility.

I acknowledge that the relative roles become harder to describe in large and more specialized organizations. But by starting with these different descriptions, it helps to understand that the two jobs are unique to nonprofit organizations and should be described and addressed as such.

The chief volunteer officer is head of the board in the fulfillment of its accountability functions. That's hardly a passive role; in unstaffed operations, it's one of sweeping proportions.

At it's simplest, the chief staff officer is hired to assist the board in its efforts to fulfill its accountability.

As the organization grows in size and complexity, other specific functions may be delegated to the chief staff officer. As this happens, the delegation should be explicit and should be reflected in the job description.

- Do you expect him or her to be the chief program officer?

- Do you expect her to be the chief spokesperson?

- Do you expect him to be responsible for fundraising?

- Do you expect her to be responsible for planning?

The board and the staff need to know whether such functions will be tightly controlled by the board or whether they will be largely delegated.

While it may seem extreme, it gets at the heart of the difficulty for many organizations to ask the questions, "Do you hold the chief staff officer responsible for fundraising or is he or she looking to you for that?" and, "If it's a shared responsibility, who does what?"

A great many of these differences can be anticipated and to some extent reduced if the job descriptions and expectations of both board and staff are clear. The misunderstandings and problems will also be minimized by the annual evaluation of the chief staff officer, which provides opportunities for catching problems early and for making adjustments. Knowing how easily the chief volunteer and staff officers can be in conflict, without any reflection on them as individuals, should create an awareness of how important it is that they work very hard at understanding one another's roles.

In a survey of board chairpersons and presidents, Robert E. Cleary concluded, "How well the chairmen and presidents work together depends less on any characteristic of the institution than on the personal factor, the degree of trust and respect the two feel for each other." He even titled his report "Something Personal About It."

At times, a controversy can divide the chief volunteer and staff officers and, if not handled well, will lead to an even greater problem than the original controversy. It is hoped that the two will be mature enough to work out their differences, or at least be willing to disagree and to have their different points of view presented for consideration and decision. It is especially hoped that maturity will allow each to handle defeat when necessary. I rarely disagree publicly with a chief volunteer officer, but I do make it very clear to each new person in that role that I have a right to do so. It is easily overlooked, particularly in the turnover of chief volunteer officers, that the chief staff officer is hired by the board and is responsible to the full board. This often becomes confused because one of the roles of the staff director is to serve as the executive assistant to the chairperson, which can lead to the misperception that one is the staff subordinate of the other. Although it is slightly presumptuous and sometimes awkward, I sit down with a new chief volunteer officer as soon as he or she is identified and, within many other matters of orientation, review my responsibility to the board. It also helps to avoid later problems if we do find ourselves in disagreement, and I think both opinions should be presented to the board.

On those rare occasions when we do disagree and can't work it through, I always suggest that we work together in presenting the whole issue to the board. Fortunately, I have never run into a situation when it was not possible to follow this arrangement. I do know, however, that in several other organizations, even with the most talented and mature chief volunteer and staff officers, there have been occasions when the two found themselves locked in controversy. In such cases it's sensible to have a third party explore the issues and then present all the issues to the governing body. This process can be useful if the controversy involves other factions in the organization, and it's particularly valuable if the differences have reached the personality level.

In "Conflict in the Board Room," J. L. Zwingle found that friction between these two positions and between the staff director and the board as a whole is a widespread cause of resignations by chief staff officers, but that neither party is likely to seek third-party help. He concluded that they ought to consider such interventions because "experience has demonstrated how even at late stages of controversy, the sense of new perspective or at least a reduction in hostility can be achieved."

The chief staff officer should not try to be in the lead on every issue that comes up. Unfortunately, too many of us tend to identify ourselves emotionally as plaintiff or defendant and are in the middle of issues that don't really require it. As a result, we become more controversial than necessary and tend to get too upset and too scarred. In an organization that truly has the capacity for controversy and dissent, you'll generally find that the staff director has a high tolerance for both and is more involved in maintaining an arena conducive to healthy controversy than in trying to win on every issue. I don't suggest a profile of timidity or passiveness, but I don't think it's healthy for the organization or the individual when the chief staff officer is expected to fight or even stand up and be counted on every issue.

Differences, debate, controversy, and dissent can all be healthy and are characteristics of vibrant citizen organizations. The organization and its structure must represent a healthy arena for the adversaries. The chief staff officer in particular must have a stomach for difference and an awareness that his or her larger job is to maintain the healthy arena rather than to take on each tiger as it comes along.

It's also important that incoming chief volunteer officers should not come at their jobs with a determination to shake things up and make a great many changes. Volunteer organizations, more than another kind of institution, get shaken up very easily. Don't start too much controversy and dissent unless the board clearly believes a total shake-up is necessary. Otherwise, pick your spots carefully and move only on those matters most in need of revision.

This chapter began by exploding the myth that boards make policy and the staff carries it out, and it ends by dispelling another myth. People often think of staff salaries as an overhead expense. Even fairly sophisticated boards become concerned if staff salaries begin to represent a high proportion of the budget. Contrary to this view, I frequently counsel boards that unless the staff salaries and other supporting expenses come above 50 percent of the budget, the agency probably is not doing a real job.

The basic program force of most citizen organizations is either: 1) the volunteers' time and energy, which moves the community toward improved attitudes and practices, or 2) the specialist staff members who provide direct services. The major cost of operating most voluntary agencies is the staff who provide day-to-day service to the volunteers or to the clients. The staff person serving a childhood mental illness committee or working to promote jobs is just as legitimate a program expense as the nurse in a hospital, teacher in a school, or minister in a church. The staff is not overhead. I certainly agree that overhead should be kept as low as possible, and if the staff is spending most of its time on fundraising or management activities, there is need for concern. But if the staff time is logged on behalf of the mission of the organization, it is program money well spent.

7

Finding, Developing, and Rewarding Good Board Members

For the head of the board, having enthusiastic and reliable board members is almost as good as having an enthusiastic spouse and reliable children, and some days, such as just before the annual board meeting, you might trade the kids two for one.

The problem is that most of us wait until those moments of crisis to give adequate consideration to solid board membership. We fail to spend time to find, develop, and reward good board members. It's like trying to build a professional football team without the efforts of scouting, signing, training, and rewarding. Our business is almost entirely people, yet we invest almost nothing in people-building. We get so tied up in today's needs that we don't reserve a realistic part of our resources for developing the talent and dedication necessary to carry and expand the association's efforts tomorrow.

The building begins with the board itself. I wish I could suggest a short cut, but I'm afraid there's no way to avoid beginning with and emphasizing the nominating committee. Businesses have their recruiters and search firms, and professional sports have their scouts; for us it's the nominating committee. The difference is that the other groups take it seriously. On the surface, almost all of us would say that the nominating committee is one of our most important committees. But if you look at the number of meetings and hours spent by committee members and staff, I'll bet the contradiction is glaring. Also, we rarely want to use some of our top talent for such a mundane function, or, if we assign them to the nominating committee, we don't want to take up much of their time this way. As a result, not much seed corn is sown.

The Association of Governing Boards of Universities and Colleges gives appropriate prominence to board development in their incisive booklet "Committee on Trustees." The author, E. B. Wilson, former head of the board at St. Lawrence University, begins:

> No committee is more vital to the performance of the governing board . . . than the committee on trustees. The governance responsibilities of independent sector boards require that trustees exercise diligent, energetic leadership and that they participate collegially in a system of shared governance. The quality of trustee stewardship of the mission and their oversight of strategic direction contribute importantly to the vigor of the institution. Few conditions are more corrosive of an institution's vitality than the inertia of a passive board of trustees.

The job begins with a careful analysis of what talent, experience, and representations are needed; this in turn requires a charting of the same characteristics of the existing board. Where do they come from? What and who (gender, age, experience, and so forth) do they represent? The nominating committee should then think hard about the imbalances and determine what skills, experience, and representations are needed to strengthen the board. At this important juncture, their ideas should be presented to the board for discussion and reaction. Often nominating committees operate in secret until their nominees are sprung full-blown on the board or voting membership. Some confidentiality is necessary when the committee reaches the state of talking about people, particularly current board members who might not be renominated, but this should not preclude an early discussion with the board about the general composition of that body.

Such a frank discussion can ease some hard feelings when favorites of current board members are not selected. Boards often tend to be self-perpetuating, not only with individuals, but also with representation of categories. It's understandable that people tend to nominate others they know, but these people are not likely to be very different than they are. I can almost guarantee that if you don't think hard about the categories and balances you need, you'll end up taking the easy course of simply choosing from among the names put forward.

Once you are fairly clear about the factors that need consideration, the board and many others can be helpful in identifying candidates who meet those criteria. One small but important point: As you involve the board and others, make it clear that they should not explore whether their people might be willing to serve. This will put you and them in an impossible spot. Interest and availability come later in the process.

When you begin to think about people, look first within the organization. The board members should represent those individuals who, in the significant majority, have proven their interest in the cause and their ability to help pursue it. The heads and members of committees should be a logical source. If yours is a membership organization, this provides an automatic pool for new board members. There is a great tendency to overleap the people who have proven themselves in hopes of getting bigger names or greater influence. My experience is that the way you build impact is to build with the people who have proven their interest.

Many boards and nominating committees want to go after the big names and new faces. After all, it makes us feel good to be serving on the board with Mr. or Ms. "Big" and to look down a bit on the organization's workers. On the other hand, one of the constant lessons of leadership is that people grow with responsibility and are capable of far more than appears on the surface. Many a leader has been amazed to discover that the people he or she has unfairly pegged at one level of output are capable of much more. An individual who has demonstrated faithful service and effectiveness at one level is the first source of leadership for higher levels of responsibility. This includes precinct captains and task force leaders who have worked faithfully and who often are overlooked for other responsibilities.

Promotion should include some deliberate turnover of top leadership. The emphasis ought to be on the development of an increasing number of persons from the lower levels who are qualified and interested in top leadership posts.

I don't suggest rapid turnover. An organization needs some people who carry forward the history and institutional culture of the organization. One sensible way to capture this is to bring people back onto the board who have served successfully and who have remained active when not on the board.

Board terms should be limited. Generally, a three-year term with a chance for renewal for an additional term makes sense. After a year off the board, a person can come back on. This recycling should be done with great caution. There is a great temptation on the part of staff and nominating committees to yearn for the good old days and past personal associations, but the larger emphasis should be on seeking new blood.

Persons who cannot be active should be dropped. My approach is to provide a clause in the bylaws that automatically drops persons who have missed a certain number of consecutive meetings, unless the board officially votes forgiveness. Letters should go annually to those board members whose attendance and participation have been irregular, indicating that in the coming year the organization will be depending more than ever on them for active participation and that if the individual board member feels that this level of participation is not possible in the immediate future, he or she can elect to step aside. I often use a sentence such as, "Obviously we very much hope you can be active, but if this is not possible, you may prefer to change your status to voting membership (supporter, inactive, and so forth) that provides continuing identification."

Joseph Reed, former staff director of the Child Welfare League, provided a good description of the qualifications of board members:

> Of greatest importance should be the person's interest in the work of the agency, commitment to its objectives, intelligence, respect in the community, capacity for growth as a board member, capacity to influence favorable public opinion in important areas of the community, ability to work in concert with others, and willingness to ask questions, offer criticism and make suggestions through proper channels.

There will be times when the nominating committee will recognize a particular need that is not yet matched by a person serving anywhere in the organization. In such cases board members must be selected from the community at large. You may know who you want and have access to him or her, know who you want but not have access, or not even know the best people who represent the leadership of that category.

Even where you have ready access, make sure that the invitation is extended in a way that the individual knows you really mean it. Send an impressive delegation. Remember that these are among the most important investments the organization will make.

Obviously the quality of the approach is even more important when you don't have easy access. With pride in your cause, ask for an appointment and bring a small group who can make it clear how important the work is. You will be amazed how often you'll not only get the appointment but an acceptance, too.

Even where the answer is no, the session can have positive results. In *Governing Boards*, Cyril O. Houle says:

> It will be comforting to realize that at least a constructive piece of community relations has been accomplished. The prospective board member will have been given information about the program, will know that he was wanted and will have sensed that the selecting authority (and probably the Board itself) knows its business. He is probably an influential person (or else he would not have been invited) and it is important to have influential people aware of the work of the agency or the association.

When you don't even know whom to ask, go to people who occupy leadership positions and seek their advice. I've often gone absolutely cold to the head of the medical society, current chairperson of the Council of Churches, publisher of the paper, head of the chamber of commerce, director of the labor council, and many others who have led me to just the right people. If it's top business leadership you are after, go to the heads of the largest businesses, making clear that you are not asking for anything but their advice. My experience is that unless you know them, you won't even get in the door if you don't offer that assurance. When you see them, present your full story and ask if there is someone else in the organization he could help you approach to make your pitch. I know you hope it will be the person with whom you are talking, but that's so unlikely that you should use the door-opening to get his or her help in enlisting someone else. If he or she suggests the executive vice president or marketing director and helps with the introduction, you will get a doubly loyal individual and will be much further ahead than if you aim unrealistically high.

The Association of Governing Boards of Universities and Colleges produced an excellent pamphlet, "Building a More Effective Board," based on a presentation by its former president, Robert Gale, in which he says:

> Generally speaking, it is not advisable to try to recruit someone who has already reached the top of the career ladder. Even if such a person accepts the invitation, he or she is likely to be too busy to contribute. It is better to look for persons who are on their way up and who are willing to work. A valuable talent for nominating committee members is the knack of identifying "comers," those who are moving up rapidly. Such persons, committed to the institution before they reach the top, become investments in the future.

Increasingly, businesses want signs that their management people are involved in voluntary endeavors and, as indicated earlier, it's my experience that people want a sense of participation and contribution. Everybody wants the corporate chief executive officer on the board, but there's a wealth of talent and commitment not far below that can be tapped.

Because I know how bewildering it can be if you don't know where or how to turn, I want to elaborate on my reference to making cold contacts. I want to reach out—almost to hold your hand—to say, "Hey, keep the faith, it can happen."

If you are really starting from scratch, I recommend starting with your political representatives. Better than anyone else, they know how the system works and who makes it work, and they usually will feel an obligation to listen and try to help. For example, they are most likely to know, say, who else has a retarded child or is worried about zoning or is concerned with improving the education system. Also, they are more likely to know who the doers are and to be able to put you in touch with some of them.

The next group I talk to are past officeholders and others who have run for office in the area. Running for and holding office require knowing a lot of people, and that knowledge is what you should quickly tap into. Incidentally, don't be afraid to make a cold approach. These people are political animals, usually easy to approach and surprisingly eager to help a fellow citizen.

My third general circle of contacts involves religious leaders. I've often gone into a community cold and, by visiting a priest, minister, or rabbi, have quickly identified people who share my concerns and people who are real doers. Those contacts serve two purposes—I not only get the names of some likely helpers, but I get automatic entrée. Very few people will not see you if you indicate that Rabbi Bloustein or Father Kelly has referred you. Often the clergyman will make the introductory call. It's amazing how helpful people will be if you dare approach them and ask for help.

The fourth group I contact are newspaper publishers, editors, and reporters who know what's happening and, while usually not so free with their time as the other groups, they still are approachable and willing to help. This can also lead to an interest in your cause and some helpful coverage.

If your community has a Voluntary Action Center (VAC) or Volunteer Bureau, talk to them. They are very good sources of volunteer leadership.

Whether it's leaders of granges, labor, business groups, media, religion, service clubs, or politics, there are people who know the individual leaders within the categories you need.

Let me repeat that board development has to be *very* high on the current board's agenda, with an awareness of how much has to be invested in it by both the board and the staff. A couple of years ago I was working with a nominating committee that had fine-tuned its analysis to the point that, for the one remaining board vacancy, they knew we needed an individual who would be from the Midwest (preferably Chicago), female, a leader of the performing arts, a volunteer (in contrast to a conductor or ballet director), an individual who had experience and interest beyond the arts, and a person who was immensely capable. That's what we needed, all in one individual! It would have been easy to consider the task impossible and even easier to give up on several of the criteria. For example, in our search we uncovered many men, many professionals, people from other sections of the country, and people from the visual arts. If we had not done our analysis so thoroughly (and there were times during that search when I wished we hadn't), we would have ended up with another male from New York and have found some way to rationalize the further imbalance. As it was, we found a remarkable individual who fit all those criteria and more.

As important as it is to be sure that the board is representative of the various constituencies and other factors necessary to the board's work, it is equally important to look for individuals who possess those human qualities that lend themselves to working as a board. I've seen organizations that tend to their needs for professional guidance, geographic and gender balance, age differential, and many other such factors, but where the nominating committee does not devote equal time to being sure that many are chosen for the board because of their proven capacity for judgment, facilitation, respect for institutional process, and just plain kindness.

I was consulted once by the organizers of a new foundation. They had pretty much identified all of the individuals who would serve on the initial board. When I looked at the list, I was dismayed that although they had covered the categories of professional expertness, they had included only individuals noted as much for abrasiveness as accomplishment. When I pointed this out, the founder countered by saying that he was determined to be different, aggressive, and innovative. I tried to make the case that such a board needed a good sprinkling of equally bright people who also had the qualities of judgment, patience, fairness, and conciliation, but he dismissed all of it as unnecessary. Two years later he was on his third executive director and four years later the foundation folded.

In all the material I've seen that assesses board makeup in any depth at all, the only points relate to specific skills and representations and pay no regard to the human qualities that in the end will make the difference in whether it's a board or a barrel of tigers. Maybe that's why so many boards get into such awful trouble. It's another argument for choosing people from within the organization who have not only proven their commitment and ability, but who have also demonstrated attractive human qualities.

When the nominating committee's annual work is done, and new board members have been elected, the process of their development begins. The orientation phase will obviously have begun with recruitment, but it should now begin to move into high gear. Even though there may be a lapse of several months between their acceptance and election, board nominees should begin to get all the regular board mailings. I also make sure they are signed up as early as possible for an orientation session. These orientation sessions serve many purposes, not the least of which is giving the newcomers a chance to get to know the organization's leadership and to know that the leadership thinks enough of them to take this special time. I make sure that the chief volunteer and staff officers conduct the orientation. Often it's delegated to others, and that larger value is lost.

Another problem with many orientation sessions is that they try to cram too much information into a session. My solution is to use a good part of the session to acquaint these important individuals with the board manual and to let them become familiar and comfortable with the agenda and attachments for their first board meeting. By focusing on the board manual, they learn what their resources are and where to find them. Thus, they don't have to be told about every program and committee of the organization, but they know where the committee chart and lists are and on what tab they can find a current summary of major program activities. By spending some time on the board meeting agenda, they get a quick grasp of what the current issues are, why they are on the agenda, and what points about them are likely to surface. This gives them a head start and makes them feel less like outsiders when the actual meeting takes place.

The board manual should cover everything from the history of the organization to the policy and procedures of covering expenses for board and committee meetings. In between there should be bylaws, policies and important procedures, organization charts, board list (including, if possible, brief bios and maybe even pictures), committee lists, staff organization chart with a summary of functions, current annual report, summary of major program activities, established dates for board and annual meetings, and the home telephone numbers of the chief volunteer and staff officers. I try to choose loose-leaf notebooks with pockets on the inside of both the front and back covers that give the board member expansion possibilities for other materials, pamphlets, and reports.

It's important that a member of the nominating committee or another board person be assigned as the host for at least the first board meeting. Some organizations assign a more permanent "buddy." At the very least, the host should call the new board member in advance of the first meeting and arrange to be available for introductions. It's a nice touch to have the host do the introductions at the beginning of the board meeting. Having to prepare for that helps the old-timer focus on the responsibility and the individual.

One of the most useful parts of orientation will begin with the new board member's assignments. It's disillusioning to be invited to serve on the board and to join with great anticipation only to be pretty much ignored. Harold Seymour says in *Designs for Fund Raising* that, "Most people don't drop out from overwork. They drop out from boredom."

Often the conscious phase of board development is limited to the initial orientation. While most of this book is about board development, a few points should be underscored here. Orientation should be aimed at all board members and, to every extent possible, should be a part of each board meeting. We some-how assume that trustees have an overview of what's happening, which isn't likely. It's important to take the time to give them the fun and the value of know-ing what's going on.

Board development is achieved in the same way that people are developed in their other roles, such as in their day-to-day work. It's largely a result of their being given the chance to do new tasks along with reasonable amounts of train-ing and on-the-job supervision. In many cases, this involves the board head being available to provide that kind of responsible leadership. Often we throw volunteers into new assignments on a sink-or-swim basis and then wonder why they're not doing well.

If board members are given a role in planning and evaluation, and if board meetings represent a forum for fulfillment of board accountability and leader-ship, both the new and current members will be growing in responsibility, knowledge, and pride. They will also be developing as a cohesive unit. In *Governing Boards*, Houle says:

> Proper attention to motivation is also essential after people have joined the Board—if the Chairman accepts existing motives and acts skillfully and subtly in terms of them, giving the members a sense of satisfaction about what they do for the agency or association, he can gradually build responsibility on the part of individuals and enthusi-asm on the part of the group. . . . It is his job to foster such a unity of purpose and such a loyalty to objectives that each individual realizes that his own judgment is a part of the collective wisdom of the Board.

Board development also involves weeding out those who aren't perform-ing. This begins with dropping inactive board members, but it also involves dropping heads of committees who aren't doing the job. Some people say, "You can't fire a volunteer," but that's not so. People who aren't performing should be given the chance to step aside and, in the extreme, must be asked to make way for someone who is ready to perform. If a bad situation is allowed to linger, it doesn't create a good atmosphere for others in the organization and certainly doesn't encourage up-and-coming volunteers to feel that this is a place they want to make their commitment. It has been my experience that the person who is not performing, and who's had all the proddings and hints you will have given, will be much more relieved than hurt to be taken off the spot.

This brings us to recognition of good board members and other volunteers. Promotion is 50 percent of recognition and reward. More than plaques and pins and pats on the back, people want to know that those they respect think they're ready for bigger things. That's enormously satisfying.

Good leaders don't wait until their best people retire or even until the annual meeting to provide regular encouragement and recognition. Presidents and committee heads should regularly say by phone and notes things like, "Just wanted you to know how impressed I was with . . ." or "I know I said it the other day, but I wanted to repeat what an absolutely great job you did. . . ." Find occasions to involve these people in board meetings so that they have the fun and pride of telling the whole board what has been happening, and the board can say, "Well done."

The pins and plaques and scrolls are important, too. And don't be afraid to spend some money on them. It appalls me that organizations that benefit from thousands, if not hundreds of thousands of dollars worth of volunteer time balk at spending more than five dollars for a recognition gift. I'm with volunteers a great deal in their offices and homes and know how much these mementos mean. Despite the warped frames, curled paper, or amateurish calligraphy, the awards remain proudly displayed.

Many organizations such as the Red Cross and Boy Scouts have elaborate systems for keeping service records and providing acknowledgment of years of participation and impact. Some staff members feel that this takes up too much time and isn't really necessary, but they don't know much about human beings: To paraphrase an old saying, "Volunteer recognition is too important to be left to the staff." Periodically, a volunteer task force should look at the recognition program to be sure that it's being observed and updated.

Recognition should include particular attention to the retiring board member. Often he or she is allowed to drift off without true recognition of how much those six years have meant both to the organization and to the individual. When I was with the National Mental Health Association, all board members who had served the maximum of two consecutive terms received a gold key suitable for recasting as a pin, tie-clip, or part of a key chain. It was a tangible way of saying thanks. They also continued to receive newsletters, annual reports, and notices of annual meetings.

I always suggest to outgoing chief volunteer officers that they provide some memento for the officers and committee heads with whom they've worked. Very often this is small—something like a paperweight, personalized with the organization's logo and the individual's name, that conveys that the individual was part of a special team and is appreciated.

I don't know exactly what you are already doing, and therefore I'm terribly frustrated that I can't be more specific. But that doesn't stop me from being absolutely definite about the importance of finding every conceivable way of saying "thanks" or "you're great" or "it's been special."

Tangible acknowledgments of participation are an important part of keeping the dream alive, which I maintain is the most important function of both the volunteer and the staff leader in any voluntary enterprise.

8

Recruiting, Encouraging, and Evaluating the Chief Staff Officer

Selection of the chief staff officer of a nonprofit organization is clearly the most important decision the board of a larger association makes. For this reason, and because recruitment is handled inadequately so often, the subject deserves a chapter of its own.

It's my experience, born of many sad lessons, that it takes a unique person to succeed in the staff role of a voluntary agency. Over the years, I've developed a profile that helps me screen persons who are exploring staff possibilities. My current profile of the persons most likely to succeed is as follows:

> **They're committed to public service.** This is more than a generalization. The persons who succeed will face many rocky times. They'll be underpaid for their ability, and they'll put up with a great deal of conflict. For these reasons and many more, these persons must have a dedication to public service that will get them over these obstacles and tough times.

They like people and get along well with them. Liking people is often used as the only criterion for selection and therefore can be exaggerated. In carrying responsible positions in voluntary agencies, however, most staff people deal with a wide variety of individuals and must be able to get along with them.

They have a great deal of patience and tolerance. Staff persons work with a wide variety of volunteers who are often at their most excitable pitch. The more vibrant and active an agency, the more this will hold true. A staff person must be a stable and patient human being or the emotional aspects of working together for significant goals will get out of hand.

They are mature. Psychologists define maturity as the ability to forego short-term satisfactions in favor of long-term goals. This applies to organizations as well as individuals and particularly to successful staff persons. Most goals are long range and require persistent, dogged pursuit through all kinds of difficulties. The satisfactions are rarely found on a weekly or even monthly basis. It's only as the agency looks back from a fuller perspective that the attainments are visible and the satisfactions present.

They're willing to work hard. Successful people usually work hard, and this is particularly true in the nonprofit field. There is so very much to be done, the dedication of volunteers is so high, and the number of forces to be dealt with so great that the only way to achieve success is by working awfully hard.

Search committees must recognize the size of the recruiting job. Despite general acknowledgment that recruitment of the staff head is the most important decision the board will make, recruitment is often almost casually approached. As a result, persons who are not really qualified are often selected.

A committee should be appointed by the board of directors. It is essential that a majority of the committee be composed of board members, but it can also include an able staff person or two from other agencies in the community. If there is a parent organization, a key volunteer or staff person from that group should also serve. The first task of the committee is to decide on the skills and attributes necessary. These will constitute a checklist for later interviewing and should immediately be translated into a job description, salary scale, and even advertisements if these are to be used.

In terms of salary scales, helpful information is usually available from your local United Way, your parent organization, or, if necessary, a quick survey that the chairperson of the committee can do on a confidential basis with the presidents of like agencies. Most agencies are willing to cooperate on a volunteer-to-volunteer basis, particularly if they know they will receive a summary of the findings for use in appraising their own salary scales.*

Because most people do not fit the profile of success, it is difficult to find those people most likely to succeed. I've found that the simplest way to solve this problem is to locate someone who has already demonstrated a capacity to succeed in this unique milieu. For this reason I repeatedly and doggedly advise search committees to look within the nationwide group with which you are affiliated for experienced or promising people. If that doesn't apply in your case, then I advise checking with the directors of major agencies in your area. In other words, do almost anything to find candidates who have already demonstrated a capacity to succeed in this kind of work. Having seen the grief and trouble agencies suffer as a result of hiring the wrong people, I wish I could be sitting across from you right now to make this point so strongly that you would realize how totally I have learned this lesson.

I am often told that it's better to locate a person who knows the local scene. I don't believe it. A bright, effective community organizer is going to see that local scene and develop those contacts in lightning-fast time. Indeed, he or she will not be encumbered by some of the difficulties that the local resident might face. These difficulties involve the set ways in which individuals are already perceived, such as being someone's kid sister, being associated with the North Side, having worked for the other newspaper, and so forth.

By the time you've developed your list of skills and attributes, you'll be overwhelmed by your findings that the person you need will have to be very mature, very experienced, and brilliantly able. This, in turn, will suggest an older person. But the experience of many agencies, and certainly the experience of the Peace Corps, AmeriCorps, and other groups, makes clear how fast a

---

*Larger organizations may find it helpful to explore compensation sources such as: *The NonProfit Times'* annual salary survey, 120 Littleton Road, Suite 120, Parsippany, New Jersey 07054-1803. Phone (973) 394-1800, fax (973) 394-2888, website: www.nptimes.org; *Compensation in Nonprofit Organizations, 14th Edition*, Abbot, Langer & Associates, Inc., October 2001, Crete, IL; and *Fringe Benefits and Working Conditions in Nonprofit Organizations, 5th Edition*, Abbott, Langer & Associates, Inc., September 2001, Crete, IL. Phone (708) 672-4200, fax (708) 672-4674, web site: www.abbott-langer.com.

young, dedicated person can learn and how much this dedication means in achieving success.

For many years I was involved in developing a trainee program for which we recruited young people who then received brief training prior to their first job placement in a voluntary agency setting. These individuals quickly grew to be significant staff leaders, and their youth proved to be an asset rather than a liability. This program allowed us to carefully screen people who had the attributes of success. On-the-job experience provided most of the necessary skills. My strong advice to you is to look for the person who is likely to succeed based on fitting the profile rather than finding someone whose age would seem to be an advantage.

You may find that you want to do some advertising. This can be done through newspapers, organization newsletters, professional journals, or the internet. Use advertising only when you have not been able to generate enough candidates by close examination of personnel rosters in the organization and by talking to other agency executives. When turning to advertising, deliberately slant the ads to attract persons who have had related experience. Write the ads in such a way that you screen out as many unprepared people as possible; otherwise you will be inundated with replies.

At times, professional employment services are helpful. In addition to government and private employment agencies, professional societies often have employment services of their own. My experience indicates that you need to be adamant about the kind of people you want and the kind of people you don't. These agencies, particularly the private ones, want to give their current roster of job seekers a feeling of activity and will send all kinds of unqualified candidates. I insist on advance résumés, and I never accept the employment agency's reference checking as very thorough.

Large organizations will want to explore the involvement of search firms, many of which now specialize in nonprofit organizations. I recently chaired the search committee for a large university, and the task was made far more manageable and effective through use of one of those firms. Caution should be taken to be sure you use a group that has extensive experience with nonprofits and in your specialty, such as health or arts. Otherwise, they won't know where to turn even as much as you already do.

One last word of caution on where to look. Beware of the board member who has a friend. More agencies make bad decisions because the search committees find it awkward to decide against the friend of the president or a person pushed hard by a board member. The smaller the community, the tougher this is. Board members will feel sorry for a woman newly widowed or a county commissioner unfairly defeated, and the search committee will suddenly and totally ignore common sense and/or sound procedures. The result is that the most important decision the board can make ends up being made badly. This applies also to searches by the staff director. He or she should never give in to any pressure to hire a person who doesn't fit the profile needed. This may seem fairly obvious, but many staff people find themselves deciding in favor of friends of board members because it's awkward to ignore the advice. The goal should be to hire the best possible people. The positive result of doing that will outweigh any short-term awkwardness from turning aside the importuning of anyone.

The ideal way to screen candidates is not always available. However, if it is, I urge you to take advantage of it. If you are a part of a larger organization, let the parent organization do the initial screening. Be definite with them in terms of the skills and attributes you want, and ask them to provide three or four people whom they view as ready for such an assignment.

If you don't have the luxury of a parent organization to do this and do it well, or if you're combining that process with some other searching, your next steps should be as follows:

Screen the résumés down to five to seven people, and have someone take a personal look at each candidate. If these prospects are in other cities, ask your sister organizations to take a look at the candidates or involve your board people who may travel. Members of your board may have company counterparts in those cities, which at least gives you an opportunity to know whether the person seems to live up to his or her résumé.

When the group is narrowed, do some extensive reference checking. I don't put much stock in listed references, although I do contact them and ask pointed questions. I put much more stock in my telephone conversations with past supervisors. I've learned the hard way that most references and supervisors want to be helpful to the candidate, if only to be rid of him or her. Accept that this can be the relationship and, therefore, work very hard to get down to facts. It's helpful to explain the importance of the job and the fact that contributed money will be expended to support it. On this basis, you can make clear how essential it is to get an honest picture of the candidate's qualifications. Make clear how much you are counting on the supervisor's candor. One of the points that I use is that even if the person is hired, I want to know what skills or attributes will need strengthening. This is not only truthful and helpful, it is often the key to opening up discussion of possible weaknesses.

I'm often on the other side of these reference calls and, with very few exceptions, I am appalled at how cursory the review is. As a consequence, I rarely have to be as candid as I would be if the questioning were sharp. This tells me that most people have made up their minds, but still want to go through the steps of clearance without having their decision shaken. My approach is to shake the daylights out of my judgment. I'd rather face the error at that stage than when the person is on the job. The two things, then, that you have going for you in getting a candid appraisal are: 1) the opportunity to make clear how concerned you are about spending public money well, and 2) your desire to check the supervisor rather closely on the grounds that even if a favorable decision is made, you want to know what skills and attributes you can help the candidate develop.

Do a thorough credit check on your finalist(s). Often the current supervisor won't know a person's credit problems. The last thing you want is to bring a poor credit risk into your job and town. I've known of several public scandals that shook association reputations and that could have been avoided by a simple credit check.

Some candidates stipulate that no checking be done. They make the good case that they are simply looking into a situation, and until they are sure they want to apply, they would rather not stir things up. At times you have to abide by this. Have it understood, however, that if a person does become a finalist, the checking will have to be done before anything is lined up. This stage is often skipped. You will have screened (except for the reference checking), interviewed, and decided that he or she is the best. There'll be a feeling of euphoria that you've finally located the right person, and there's no sense going through the awkwardness of postponing firming it up when you are so confident that the decision is correct. Resist closure under these circumstances until the reference checking is done. I have learned over the years that the majority of people don't succeed in this field; consequently, there are many inefficient people in it, many of whom contradict their low level of general performance by being superior at selling themselves in job interviews.

The full search committee should see the candidates, and if possible, during the span of the same day or on successive days. The group should take time to decide how they'll conduct themselves during the interviews. The committee should develop a list of skills and attributes and clear any revisions in the job description and salary scale with the board of directors. It's usually a pretty good idea to check the job description because there's no better time to change the job description than when the post is vacant.

Please, please don't play games during the interviews. I've been involved in situations where members of the committee tried to shake up the candidate or tried in other ways to "see what the candidate is really made of." That's a good way of turning off your best candidates. Approach the interview through straightforward, candid discussion of the job and the potential mismatch between the job description and the candidate. It's useful to describe real-life situations in the organization and ask the candidates almost as though they were consultants to share ideas for dealing with those situations.

It's important, too, to explain candidly any reservations the committee has about the individual in terms of gaps in experience, possible weak areas, a questionable reference check, and the like. Remember that it's a two-way proposition. Help the candidate to screen him or herself out. This is hard to do because you want to present a favorable picture. It's human nature to want people to want the job, but, on the other hand, it's better to be candid if that helps a candidate recognize that he or she is not matched for what you really want—better to learn it at this time than later. If the selection process is strung out at all, keep the candidates posted. This is a courtesy too often overlooked.

Naturally, the committee's own instincts will play a significant part in the final recommendation. It is advisable, however, to introduce some objective measures in order to check your intuition and to be certain that each candidate is being viewed in light of the same criteria. My suggestion to search committees is that they take the attributes and skills needed and set out a score sheet. I usually suggest a rating of 0 to 5, with 5 being the highest mark. It's a good idea not to use these score sheets during the interview, but, instead, to take a few minutes after each interview for the committee members to mark their score cards. Seeing all candidates on the same day, or on successive days, will bring more uniformity into this process.

After you've rated all the candidates, the committee will probably be surprised at the scores. I don't suggest that the scores will necessarily contradict instinct, but you will be fascinated that some candidates who didn't seem very impressive will come up with good scores. This leads to a much more objective discussion of the candidates in relation to the skills and attributes you are really looking for. One individual may not be terribly dynamic but, on scores, comes up pretty solid right across the board. You may still decide on the individual who has more flair, but, again, you may not. It's the scoring that will lead you to know what you're deciding.

I have had experience enough to predict that when this more orderly method is used, the committee members will end up hiring someone who would not have been their first choice if left to their own instincts. Further, I would guess that they would agree then and two years later that their instincts, to some extent, had deceived them.

I follow this process in promoting and hiring as well. There have been times when I have known for certain who the right persons were for given posts, but I still have made myself go through the exercise of trying to identify objectively skills and attributes and to rate the several people. In the end, I have found that my obvious candidates were at least surprisingly well challenged and sometimes overtaken. Good judgment is based on sound analysis, and sound analysis is based on accurate data.

The search committee reports to the board. If it is not possible for the full board to be involved in the decision, the executive committee usually has that authority. Some organizations give the search committee final authority to identify one choice and then refer the candidate to the board of directors or executive committee. I tend to favor the search committee narrowing the field to two to four people and then having the board do the final interviewing. In this case, the board or executive committee should follow the interviewing procedure outlined previously. When the process involves the full board or at least the executive committee, the most experienced people in the organization are participating. This also means that the fuller group will have some real commitment to the candidate selected.

If both the search committee and executive committee or board are involved in the interviewing, it can be done in tandem to save time and expense. For example, the search committee can see five people on Friday and refer two to the board on Saturday.

If the position involved is not that of staff director, then the choice should be entirely that of the staff person who will be responsible for the supervision. A staff person may want board members to interview a candidate just to get another perspective, but the board should not have a veto right. Similarly, the board members may be asked to help screen and interview applicants for a department head, but the final decision should rest completely with the executive director.

Follow a strict timetable for selecting an executive director. Prolonged search operations are unhealthy for the organization's morale and are unnecessarily awkward. At the local level, the process may not require more than three months, including time to determine attributes and skills, develop the job description and salary scale, and search for and screen applicants.

The agreement should indicate that there is a six-month probation period. This should apply to all professional positions. During the probation period, the new staff persons should be entitled to the basic fringe benefits. The letter confirming the appointment should cover all essential understandings, including salary, salary scale, moving costs, and starting date. The candidate should be asked to return a signed copy of the letter for the personnel records.

I am frequently asked if there should be a contract, and I almost always say no. I acknowledge that when I became executive director of the National Mental Health Association, the management consulting firm involved in the search had already written into the procedures that there would be a three-year contract. When that expired, I made no move to have it renewed. My own feeling is that a board must be free to change executive directors. If a person goes into a situation hopeful of being able to handle it, that's part of the gamble. I know this doesn't add much to job security, but I don't feel job security is an available luxury in this business. It's important to acknowledge that many experienced people in the field strongly disagree with me on the matter of contracts.

An important consideration is the matter of timing the change. Try to follow the golden rule so that you are not trying to hasten a starting date beyond what you would consider reasonable if you were losing one of your own. I do recommend that people take some time off before starting a new job. This is an important transition with a good deal of emotional and physical stress at both ends. Therefore, if at all possible, there should be at least two months between the agreement and the starting date.

It's usually helpful to have the new staff director make a trip or two to the office before starting. This can involve the person in board meetings or other major events so that, even though he or she will not start for a while, the individual can begin to get a feel for what is going on.

Please do send letters to the references, prior supervisors, and present employers of the person selected. This is a courtesy almost always overlooked and will help your own public relations. The president or the chairperson of the search committee should call the other finalists to thank them for their participation and to outline the final decision. Let the candidates ask questions about the impression they made. This can be useful to them in future situations. Finally, if the new director is from another city, he or she will profit from as much help as you can give in getting settled in and oriented to the new community.

Given the unique profile of a successful staff person and the breadth of activities encompassed by most voluntary organizations, staff turnover is very costly business. Yet most voluntary agencies still do not approach the important business of retaining good people with anything close to the priority treatment it deserves.

Holding onto good staff is neither wholly nor even largely a matter of salary and benefits. These people want a sense of purpose, contribution, and fulfillment. In *"The Motivation to Work,"* Frederick Herzberg found that achievement, recognition, work itself, responsibility, and advancement are the primary sources of job satisfaction. This is particularly true of the kind of person who tackles the staff role in a nonprofit agency.

Certainly one can't dismiss the importance of realistic salary scales and fringe benefits. These must be a part of the effort to attract, promote, and retain good people. Fringe benefits should include basic medical, major medical, and retirement coverage, and the benefits program should be transferable if a person moves within a state or national organization. The salary scale should be competitive with other agencies at a level realistic enough that the person is not constantly anguished by failure to provide basic family needs.

Various surveys indicate that nonprofit professional salaries are one-third to one-half less than those in comparable jobs in industry. (The differential is usually much greater for the top jobs.) In an important study, "Work and Workforce Characteristics in the Nonprofit Sector," Phillips Mirvis and Edward Hackett reported that "nonprofit jobs provide more challenge, variety, satisfaction and intrinsic rewards than those in private enterprise or government." Their findings indicate that these satisfactions will attract and help retain people as long as the salary differential is not more than one-third of what they could make in other sectors.

The board of directors, or at least the executive committee, should annually review an executive director's performance. The review should be based on the job description and on the executive director's role in assisting the board to carry forward the association's work. Most organizations overlook the need for an annual review; in fact, no evaluation is done until the point of brinkmanship is reached. The performance of the executive director should be measured in relation to the job description, her or his effectiveness in working with the board to fulfill the annual plan, similar effectiveness in helping the board with its accountability standards, and her or his ability to contribute to expanded volunteer involvement and responsibility.

The evaluation should take up a substantial part of the time of an executive committee or board meeting. I don't believe that this critical responsibility should ever be delegated to a personnel committee.

The review should not include evaluation of staff persons other than the executive director. Although the evaluation automatically has to cover staff performance in general, the executive director should be given absolute authority for the annual evaluation of other staff members.

Unless this matter is taken seriously, it will be given only cursory attention. The executive committee or board should take at least an hour because it takes time before the members feel comfortable and will discuss shortcomings. Even if the executive director's performance is tops, it is still important that small problems be caught before they compound into larger problems.

I predict that most evaluations will follow this pattern: For the first few minutes, there will be silence. In the next ten minutes, there will be laudatory statements. After about twenty minutes, someone will finally raise a point, such as, "I know he works hard, but I'm not sure what he does all that time." The session obviously should not be nitpicking, but it should be thorough enough so that, if members have concerns about performance, they will come out and be discussed objectively. At times, this process indirectly solves other relationship problems. A member of the board may be laboring under a misperception of the executive director's role or handling of a given situation, and, once it's brought up, the misunderstanding may be dispelled. The president should take time after the meeting to review the report, including items of commendation and areas for improvement. It should be a growth situation for the individual and, therefore, for the organization.

Throughout this book I've talked about the importance of volunteers and boards and the essentially subordinate role of staff, but none of that is to deny the importance of good staff. Far more of the voluntary organization's planning and resources should go to building and nurturing good staff.

9

Constructive Planning— Even in Voluntary Organizations

A good description of planning in voluntary organizations can be summarized as, "We'll do as much good as we possibly can and that's all we can do." There is somehow an assumption that because the mission is so large and the purposes so important it is not possible, nor perhaps even humane, to define what is most important, especially if this means conscientiously deciding that certain important purposes will not be addressed.

One of the principal results of trying to accomplish more than is attainable is that all accountability is lost. It's not possible to expect or require someone to be finished with a task by next Friday or April 30 if the individual can come back and say that he or she is so swamped with other assigned tasks that there is no way this new task can be done. Presidents and executive directors of organizations start out each year with such sweeping expectations that as the months pass, and it becomes obvious that most of these expectations can't be fulfilled, there is a tendency to get discouraged and to begin hoping that next year might be different.

In the absence of more realistic planning, most voluntary agencies are governed, and badly so, by the *bright idea*. A president, committee chairperson, board member, or staff member gets a bright idea about what should be done and off the agency zags. The organization is almost defenseless against the bright idea because it sounds so good or might help so many people, but there is no mechanism to put it in competition with all the other things that might be done. The board in particular may be frustrated because most of its members aren't close enough to really know what's going on, and they can't quite grasp where the agency is and why and what is already being done.

What planning is taking place may be related only to what the staff thinks the agency should be doing. This is another example of the way agency control drifts or is pulled in the direction of staff dominance. Many thoughtful volunteers have concluded that planning is always going to be a staff role because only staff members have the necessary continuity, overview, and time to plan. I don't agree. Indeed, I think if the board can't be put in charge of planning, the volunteer character of the organization is considerably weakened.

The board is responsible for planning and must vote on the actual plans. This function can be assigned to a board committee and, in the case of multi-year plans, certainly should be. There may be a great deal of delegation to the staff, but this should only be to facilitate the board's work. Plans and evaluation of performance in relation to them are what the board is accountable for.

One of the problems of effective board involvement in planning is that people, particularly planners, always make planning seem so complicated. I've consulted with planning officers of large corporations to try to improve my own approach to planning, only to be put off by the jargon and makework of what to me is an unnecessarily complicated process.

It is reasonable to engage in an intelligent approach to planning without having the process use up all available time. For several years I participated in annual "planning retreats" designed to give an organization's officers an opportunity to effectively decide where they want to be a year hence. I've used this process at the local, state, and national levels, and in all cases have found it to have tremendous benefits.

The process of an annual planning retreat begins with the president asking board members, committee chairpersons, staff members, and others what they consider to be the most important tasks to accomplish in the current year. These are carefully catalogued for advance study by the officers. The agency's top volunteer and staff leaders then go into a one or two-day concentrated planning session designed to identify, but not to undertake, the major projects and goals for the year and to determine to whom they will be assigned. The object of the planning retreat is to develop what I call the annual agenda—the organization's carefully planned objectives—for the year ahead. If the agency has had an opportunity to develop its multi-year goals, the annual agenda should, of course, relate to them.

A typical agenda for an officers' planning retreat should, then, include these topics:

- Review of our mission.

- Review of our current resources.

- What did we get done in the past twelve months?

- What didn't we get done?

- Review of our continuing responsibilities.

- What *has* to be done in the next twelve months?

- Can we get it done?

- What it's going to take?

- What important projects can't we do next year?

- Can we get the board to agree?

- Who's going to be responsible for what?

If yours is a typical group, this process will represent the first time your leadership group will have gained a common perception of what's most important to do and what can't be done.

As a starter, it will be revealing and useful to have each individual privately list the two or three most important things he or she would like to see accomplished in the year ahead. While these are being recorded and tabulated, ask the group to list the assets or strengths of the association. These simple approaches will help set the stage for some very solid planning. The group, as a group, will begin to have a common grasp of the mission, where the organization stands, and an appreciation of the diverse expectations of its leaders. This should quickly lead to the heart of the session, which is to decide what is *in fact* possible and what is *really* most important.

The process of holding an annual planning retreat has benefits far beyond even the significant advantage of gaining a clear idea of where you're going. For instance, the very nature of the session provides the officers with a common grasp of existing commitments and resources. Also, by being involved in the planning, the officers feel a commitment to the goals for the year. These factors increase their capacity for teamwork and reduce the many frictions and breakdowns in communication that could later occur.

One of the most exciting aspects of these planning retreats is the camaraderie that develops. We sometimes forget that the volunteer officers, even if they live in the same neighborhood or city, often don't know one another very well and frequently have quite different perceptions of the organization. By hammering out the difficult decisions about how to utilize limited resources, the individuals really come together as a group. The planning retreats are not easy sessions; properly organized, they should be designed to decide what *not* to attempt to accomplish or what should be assigned low priority, which obviously means that some individuals will be disappointed. However, through more than forty years of this process at the local, state, and national levels, I have never known a case where the end result was not a tightly knit and enthusiastic team.

Still another advantage of the planning retreat is that the individuals in the organization come out of the session and the subsequent board meeting on the offensive—that is, they know where they want to go, and they're determined to get there.

One of the real advantages of the resulting annual agenda is that it provides the board and staff with an ability to say no to all the bright ideas that come along during the year. On the other hand, if an idea or project that competes with their carefully determined goals obviously needs to be dealt with, the officers and board can make a conscious decision about it. It's amazing that even after going through this involved process, one of the tough jobs of the organization is to stay on course. If an association is dealing with a critical public problem, there will be many calls for a reappraisal of decisions and many new proposals for priority effort, but at least the process of the planning retreat and the existence of the annual agenda provide ammunition for staying the course.

The existence of an annual agenda makes the whole organization more aware of the need to accomplish the most important tasks. There should be reports to the executive committee and board of directors involving the volunteer leaders responsible for each of the areas of activity, and everyone should know that progress is being charted.

It's a good idea to print your annual agenda on large posters to be available at board meetings. If your board and committees generally meet in one place, affix a set of these posters to the wall and, if possible, show the degree of fulfillment to date. These devices may sound terribly managerial and, indeed, are foreign to most voluntary agencies, but unless citizen groups learn to identify the most important things to be done and then find ways to lock in resources to accomplish them, they will continue to be characterized as inefficient do-gooders.

During the process of the annual retreat and in the board's later consideration of the resulting recommendations for the annual agenda, the following guidelines might be useful.

- **Keep the meeting focused.** The more you search, the larger the focus can become. That's also a way of avoiding saying no. During some of your debates, you and the others won't want to see certain activities voted down, and the temptation will be to say, "Well, that's really a part of D (which, of course, it won't be at all), so let's just make it part of that priority." Don't do it.

- **Keep the plan simple.** For example, don't assume that a new committee or a task force is needed. On many matters your central group should act as a committee of the whole. As the operation grows, decentralization may be necessary, but a good rule is to respond to that only when there is no alternative.

- **Keep the meeting action-oriented.** Trustees are tired of being involved in organizations that seem to be caught up in maintaining themselves or that are too timid to act. It is hoped that you have enlisted people who want to make a difference in a specific area; if they sense and see that you and the operation are action-oriented, you'll hold the best of them.

- **Involve the group in deciding the attainable goals and the methods for achieving them.** This process requires the genuine involvement of the officers and board members, as well as staff. If this is reduced to a discussion of only specific recommendations served up to the board without their prior participation, you may get approval, but you are not likely to get followership. Two meetings hence, when people propose new program priorities, you'll wonder where they were when the program plan was approved.

- **Make your goals specific.** Goals and strategies for achieving them should be very specific. In your fact-finding stage, pin down exactly what must happen to bring about the desired results and how you can make it happen.

- **Don't assume that your organization has to go it alone.** There may well be other groups who are interested in the same results. Part of your planning should involve the networking necessary to build allies and the specific plans for those negotiations. Decide what your best course or strategy should be. You can picket, boycott, expose, sue, establish, elect, fund, lobby, shame, demonstrate, augment, or whatever else will bring about the change or service you seek. The more specific you can be in defining the problem, goal, and strategy, the more rapidly you'll see results.

- **Condition yourself and the group to keep the faith if it's likely to be a long-term effort.** John W. Gardner has observed that "the first requirement for effective citizen action is stamina." It's almost certainly not going to be easy. For that reason, it's essential to latch on to every evidence of progress and to be sure that the board is given full opportunity to know that the effort is getting somewhere and that they have the right to be encouraged and to rejoice in the evidence of their growing effectiveness.

- **Remember that people are very generous toward important public causes.** You have the encouragement of knowing in advance that if you are really willing to work at it, you can raise the money necessary to achieve your goals.

Most of what I've described represents an effort on the part of the current officers to gain a grasp of where they want to be at the end of their term and to have some means of locking in resources to get there. Several times, however, I've referred to the relationship of this process to the multi-year goals of the agency. Here, too, I don't want to scare you off with the complexities of a process, but obviously an agency dealing with a longer-term effort should have an idea where it wants to go over the course of at least the next several years. This process, too, should involve and emphasize board participation and responsibility. It, too, doesn't have to be terribly complicated; indeed, most things come down to common sense and some rudimentary skills.

In the area of multi-year planning, a volunteer group should be assigned to take a careful look at the mission of the organization, its current goals, the progress toward those goals, and the available resources. This, in turn, will help the board think about what is most important to be done six and seven years hence. A good deal of time should be allowed for the process so that there can be plenty of give-and-take about what the various elements of the organization believe are important. This process may spark some intense debates and perhaps cause upset; however, in the end, the membership and board will have had an opportunity to think through where they've been, where they are, and where they're going, along with what they consider to be the most promising steps for moving closer to the fulfillment of the agency's mission.

There are, of course, still more sophisticated levels of planning, involving such things as quantification of goals, but my experience has been that professional planners usually scare voluntary agencies away from sensible beginnings by making planning sound more involved than it really needs to be. Obviously, it's wise to take advantage of solid experience in any specialty, including planning. However, select someone who knows your organization and who is realistic. Most planners want to immediately bring the organization to a level of sophistication far beyond the time or resources that can be assigned.

Even as you move into more complex planning, the process and results must never be beyond the board's grasp and control. Be sure that you, as a board member, understand what is behind such terms as *strategic planning*, *needs assessment*, and *management by objectives*. Most of it comes down to common sense approaches to deciding what's most important to be done, what resources are necessary, how to divide up the tasks, and how to evaluate progress. In *Managing for Impact of Nonprofit Organizations: Corporate Planning Techniques and Applications*, James M. Hardy deals with the important technicalities that help a voluntary organization carry on the kind of planning now fairly routine in large business corporations. Much of this is accomplished in four levels.

Hardy points out that initially the board should articulate the "ideal goals." Essentially this is the statement of purpose usually covered in the certificate of incorporation or bylaws. According to him, it is "a description of the ideal or reason for existence of the organization. It frequently defines the organization's ethical tone and basic philosophy, but is never completely attainable. Ideal goals are usually infinite and consequently they tend to be a relatively fixed organizational anchor point."

His second level involves the "corporate goals," which he says constitute ". . . a description of the desired future that is possible and that provide definite direction for the total organization. These goals are formulated through a process that is directed by the Chief Executive Officer, approved by the Board of Directors and become the 'planning umbrella' within which all operating units accomplish their annual planning. The time span for corporate goals is usually five years. Each corporate goal frequently has a related statement of expected outcomes; that is, a description of the kinds of conditions that will exist in five years if the corporate goal has been satisfactorily achieved."

His third level constitutes the ". . . objectives—specifically measurable statements of attainable outcomes within the framework of the corporate goals. Objectives are developed by operating units. The time span for objectives is usually one year."

The fourth level is made up of the ". . . action steps, specific work segments, or activities necessary for the achievement of objectives. The time span is usually one to twelve months."

In the *Strategic Planning Workbook for Nonprofit Organizations*, written by Bryan W. Barry for the Amherst H. Wilder Foundation, the planning task is divided, and later detailed, in five stages:

1. "Getting Organized," including deciding to develop a strategic plan; selecting a group or person to coordinate the effort; outlining a planning process; enlisting any outside help; getting necessary approval to proceed.

2. "Taking Stock (situation analysis)," including pulling together necessary background information such as review of mission, existing goals, and results to date.

3. "Setting Direction," including: identifying critical issues for the future; clarifying the organization's mission; identifying future focus, goals, and general strategy; and preparing a discussion draft of a possible plan.

4. "Refining and Adopting the Plan," including: discussions with many stakeholder groups and other knowledgeable persons to get good reactions, suggestions, and ideas for implementation; preparing revised drafts to reflect those discussions ("the result of your review should be a plan that is both sound and doable—a plan that people understand and are committed to implementing"); and gaining adoption and commitment from the board and, if you are a membership organization, from the Membership.

5. "Implementing the Plan," including: translating the plan into yearly work plans and budgets; keeping focused on the big goals, staying at it, and monitoring progress.

Wilder's Workbook very wisely adds one other essential feature of successful plans, and that is, "A plan which has heart . . . in which participants speak candidly about their hopes for the organization and what it can accomplish, their commitments, and other matters of heart. A strategic plan has little power if it is disconnected from people's hopes and commitments. The difference between an adequate plan and a great plan is often around these matters."

Many voluntary organizations are moving into strategic planning, including churches, scouts, museums, orchestras, colleges, and health agencies. The sophistication of their processes and plans is encouraging, but unfortunately some of these agencies give the impression that any organization that hasn't reached their level of planning competence isn't really doing strategic planning. That's nonsense. A family that knows its values, decides its priorities, and budgets its income is still one of the best examples of strategic planning. And there's probably a lot less slippage in that unit than in a more sophisticated organization.

Don't be put off, but don't put it off. Keep in mind the maxim, "If you don't know where you're going, you'll end up someplace else." I would add that, in a voluntary agency, if you don't know where you're going, you'll end up zigzagging in all directions. But, if the board has used a common-sense approach to figure out what the resources are and how best to assign them, you're more likely to end up with a giant step in the direction of the organization's basic purpose.

10

Working with Committees

Be kind to committees. They are our most maligned organizational species. For every person who says with pride, "I got appointed to the committee," there are a thousand who put it, "You won't believe what they've done to me!" The jokes abound:

- An elephant is a horse designed by a committee.

- A committee keeps minutes and wastes hours.

- The best committee has three members—with two always out of town.

- A committee is made up of the unfit trying to lead the unwilling to do the unnecessary.

- A committee is a collection of individuals who separately do nothing and together decide that nothing can be done.

I suppose that raises a question about having committees at all. Committees do serve a purpose, although I will say that I believe in the "principle of least number." The board of directors should handle as many matters as possible. Also, the work of many committees, including such subjects as bylaws, can usually be accommodated by ad hoc assignments as needed. I am a great believer in "adhocracy." All committees, except those required and identified in the bylaws, should be ad hoc, including the stipulation that they automatically go out of business at the end of the year unless specifically recharged by the board. Cyril O. Houle, in *Governing Boards*, recalls the quip, "To have one committee is better than to have two, to have two is better than to have three, and so on. It is all too clear what would be better than one committee."

I am also a great user of one-person task forces, or at least few-person task forces, which are asked to do their business in one or two meetings and then automatically go out of business.

It is standard practice today for all kinds of organizations to go through the exercise of starting with a blank slate. If there were no committees, which ones would you actually recreate, and are there other ways to do the same business?

You may want to write down the functions that must be performed and then decide on the simplest way of carrying out those jobs. Such functions might include bylaws, personnel, finance, annual meeting, fundraising, public relations, awards, nominating, legal, program(s), emergency decisions, and other necessary business between board meetings.

When I was chief staff officer of INDEPENDENT SECTOR we didn't have an executive committee. There was strong feeling on the part of the organizers that executive committees tend to consolidate decision-making among too few people and end up doing the work of the board while leaving out most of the trustees. It's amazing how few matters really can't wait for the next board meeting and how easy it is to fall into the easier pattern of using the smaller group. The classic situation is that the executive committee usually deals with the executive director's evaluation and compensation, and the board isn't even told what the staff director is paid.

When emergency matters arise, there usually isn't time for an executive committee meeting, so that, too, is not a terribly valid rationale. We followed the procedure that the chief volunteer officer, chief staff officer, and head of the committee of reference could make a necessary decision on behalf of the organization as long as it did not contradict an existing policy or other decision already passed by the board. I cite this simply as an example of the fact that it is possible to challenge the traditional thinking about committee structure.

I realize that for many organizations an executive committee is an important instrument of decision-making. Such committees are usually able to exercise all the powers of the board except changes in the bylaws. This creates the danger of the executive committee functioning in place of the board of directors, but some think that practicalities necessitate that risk.

If you have an executive committee it should be large enough to be representative of the board. It should not be simply the officers and one or two others. Some executive committees include the officers and committee chairpersons. I advise against this because it puts together a group too easily given to pork barreling and not equipped to give an objective review of emergency matters coming before it.

Executive committee minutes should be circulated quickly to all board members, and each board meeting should include a report of executive committee actions. This all too rarely happens, and the board doesn't have much opportunity to ask why these matters were not postponed until the board meeting. The usual excuse is that the matters were too complex for the full board. Look behind that to see if it really is so, and even when it is, ask why the board didn't at least have a chance to vote on the executive committee's recommendation.

In the name of simplicity, INDEPENDENT SECTOR had a management committee, which consolidated the personnel, finance, audit, equal opportunity, and other management oversight functions. Our nominating and awards functions were also consolidated. Legal issues were handled by the program committee involved or by the management committee. Bylaws revisions were an ad hoc function. On the other hand, fundraising was a very distinct committee function, one that I would never combine with public relations or another assignment. It's always too easy to get diverted into other less concrete functions and to postpone the urgent task related to the fundraising plan and its implementation.

Having argued for simplification, let me make what could appear to be a contradictory point. When a committee is needed, I don't argue the "principle of least number." If such a group is in fact needed, then it must include ample involvement from the various forces and interests within the organization and community. If you are convinced the function is necessary, be sure that all who need to be involved in the decisions and their implementation are members. I'm speaking primarily of program and policy issues that have broad implications for your organization and its constituencies.

Except for the nominating committee, the chief volunteer officer should have full authority to appoint chairpersons and committees. Heads of committees should have an opportunity to request a few people they feel are essential to the task, but it is the volunteer president who needs to make all the appointments. This is necessary to be sure that certain individuals are not overused and others underused and to be certain that the organization is reaching out to all the individuals and groups that should be involved. For committees, I don't believe in staggered terms, at least as stipulated by policy or bylaw. This restricts the opportunity of a president to make significant changes when they are needed. Instead, the president should informally stagger the appointments in order to achieve a balance of experience and new blood.

Unless it doesn't make sense for the task at hand, committees and task forces should include a mix of board members and others. Spread the work and the opportunities; it's a good way to develop future board members and officers.

The chief volunteer officer should serve ex officio as a member of all the committees of which he or she has appointment authority; this should be so also for the committee head who appoints subcommittees and task forces. Incidentally, many people assume that the term *ex officio* means participating without vote. Actually it means participating by virtue of one's office, and that role automatically carries with it a right to vote except where otherwise prohibited.

Every committee, ad hoc committee, and even subcommittee and task force should have a written charge. It's almost always an erroneous assumption that people have a common understanding of the task to be accomplished. At least once a year the committee should review its charge. I go so far as to put it in the resource materials, which are part of the committee packet sent to the group in advance of *each* meeting. It's amazing how often it is the key to bringing the group back on track.

It will greatly improve attendance and the quality of your discussions and decisions if the agenda and related materials are sent at least ten days in advance of committee meetings. It is important to underscore here that this is rarely done and is a large factor in the inefficiency of so many committees.

It's my standard practice to begin each committee meeting with an overview of current activities within the organization. Staff members fight this. Committee heads sometimes feel that it interferes with getting on with the business at hand, but committee members love it. For most of them, it's the only time that they find out how their activities relate to the organization as a whole and what has happened in the fulfillment of the organization's mission. It's a key part of giving meaning to volunteering and keeping the dream alive.

Presidents and boards should not underestimate how much staff time goes into effective service of committees and task forces. Boards, executive committees, and other committees tend to find that an easy way to deal with conflict is to refer the matter to an existing committee or to create a new one. I regularly ask boards whether they are doing this because they really want the matter handled that way, or whether it's an excuse to avoid coming to grips with the situation. Board meetings and annual meetings should provide an arena for reasonable conflict and resolution of differences. It's better to have a matter done with if this is really the intent than to prolong the process to be polite or to avert conflict. If people know how much work is entailed in establishing and servicing such unnecessary appendages, or if they recognize that it cuts into the time available to pursue real priorities, they are likely to be more hard-headed and to adopt a more sensible approach. Obviously there are times when the conflict can reach the destructive level, and, therefore, it's worth the price to keep the subject alive at the committee level. I urge only that you be aware that the price is not small.

The board should be careful to see that committee activity is pointed toward the established *program* priorities and *program* plan of the organization. It's easy to get caught up in *organizational business*. For instance, bylaws committees often take up more time than any other committee. Everyone is interested in bylaws, even when it's difficult to get these same people moving on priority fundraising and program matters. In the matter of committees, I invoke the apt phrase, "Keep your eye upon the donut and not upon the hole."

Committees tend to be better at thinking up activities than pursuing them. It's far more fun to consider what needs to be done than to get on with the decisions already made about what must be done. As a result, committees—and boards, too—tend to be "add-oners" rather than implementers. In one organization with which I worked, this became such a source of frustration and misunderstanding that I went back over the minutes of several committees and pulled out all of the decisions made. Then I matched these against the follow-through achieved and against the staff resources available to the committees. Not surprisingly, there was a startling disparity between expectations and resources, and it became obvious why the committees were upset that so many of their bright ideas had not taken hold. It didn't dawn on them that *they* were equally responsible for implementation. They had had the fun of deciding what should be done but had shirked responsibility for following through. We instituted a report, called "Summary of Past Actions," on which each decision of the committee was recorded. The third item of every committee meeting's agenda, immediately following the "Overview of Association Activities" and the minutes, was the "Summary of Past Actions." The committee members had to take a look at what they had already decided should be done and the state of implementation before going on to other business. This automatically led to a focus on things already decided rather than on new ideas.

In terms of structure, it's necessary to deal with the issue of auxiliaries. They can be a wonderful addition to an organization's fundraising and community outreach, but they can take on a life of their own. For example, on the disparity between the resources and expectations, auxiliaries can often make decisions requiring extensive staff time without regard to the organization's other expectations. For this and other reasons, I generally advise against having any part of the structure free from the obligations and constraints faced by the other parts. It comes back to the matter of simplicity. Don't establish any more complexity than is absolutely necessary.

On this point Houle says:

> But the headaches which can be created by a multiple board system are both numerous and difficult to cure. An auxiliary board may gain a great deal of prominence and prestige, and be confused in the public mind—or, worse, in its own—with the Board where the controlling power lies. An auxiliary board may gradually take on more and more functions until it exactly parallels the Controlling Board; in such a case, there is in effect a two-house legislature and every issue must be carried through both boards, to the eventual despair of the Executive. Two boards may crawl, or become deadlocked, or have any other kind of difficulties imaginable, all to the detriment of the service or program they are supposed to guide and aid.

So much for structure. What comfort and guidance are there if you should find yourself not only on the committee, but head of it? For comfort, I can only pass along the advice given to a friend who was active in civil rights efforts back in the sixties, but who, because he came in constant touch with a great many angry people, found himself roundly criticized for what he had not done. He was complaining to a friend that these people didn't seem to appreciate or give him credit for at least being well out in front of most others on these issues. He admitted to being hurt that he was not being embraced for his good works. His friend provided this advice: "Harry, if it's affection you need, get yourself a dog."

Involvement in crucial issues may not bring Harry and you much immediate affection, but you can be sure that someday you will look back on these as among the very best days of your life. It is true, after all, that service is its own reward.

Much of what is true of the role of the president applies to you and your important sphere of activity. You're the one who must encourage, applaud, prod, and even "fire and hire." Although the chief volunteer officer has the ultimate authority for committee appointments, you have every right to ask for a few people you believe are important to the task and with whom you feel particularly comfortable. Also, you have a right to ask that certain individuals not be appointed or reappointed.

It's your job to see that the committee is as good at implementation as it is at blue-skying. This means giving plenty of time to creativity but at least equal time to hitching the team to those dreams. No matter how much you rely on staff, you're responsible for the committee, including such mundane things as approval of the agenda and related resource material, and making sure that they are mailed to the committee far enough in advance of meetings for adequate study. You are ultimately responsible for the accuracy of minutes.

Beyond the important mechanics and other details, your basic job is to build a team equal to the task and to give them a sense of being a team. Step back periodically to evaluate your performance, not only in terms of decisions made and their implementation, but whether the group is coming together in a way that will allow for even greater achievement. That includes respect for the group and a willingness to really let it contribute rather than merely respond to your bright ideas or those of staff members. I recall being named to a committee of quite impressive performers who, because of the importance of the task and the quality of persons named, showed up in force at the first meeting. Then, in the form of his opening statement, the chairman threw this bucket of ice water on us, "I do so hope you all agree with me that the course we should follow is . . . ." That was thirty years ago, but I still recall it vividly. On the other hand, I can't recall anything else about it. I never went back.

In "Better Boards and Committees," a pamphlet by the Adult Education Association of the U.S.A., there's a good description of the personal characteristics of the effective committee head:

1. one who has a personal record of being a consistent worker who completed a job;

2. is enthusiastic;

3. has background knowledge of the organization's aims and the committee's functions;

4. is hard working;

5. is good humored;

6. is quick;

7. is a good executive; and

8. is persuasive.

In addition, the effective committee head:

1. has confidence in other members;

2. wants to release the potential energy of the group;

3. is willing to give up the Chairman's initial prerogatives, if the job requires it; and

4. is more interested in the Committee's job than in his own feeling of personal importance.

The pamphlet concludes with: "The good chairman is one who can work with people, who can stimulate them rather than brow beat them and can help the group use all the abilities and experiences its members possess and new ones, too, that they develop as they work together."

It is important to continually give the group a sense of where they fit in. For example, show them how they fit into the scheme of the organization's overall mission and current priorities, and find ways to give them a sense of pride and accomplishment. From time to time ask the chief volunteer officer to come by, if for no other reason than to "show the flag." Take some time at meetings to bring in people who can help provide a broader perspective and some aware-ness of how their relatively small role relates to the broader roles of, say, build-ing the best museum or finding the answer to heart disease.

Every now and then, perhaps once a year, provide some social activity. It might help remind you to do this if you think that the committee should have its own annual meeting. On those occasions be sure there's a combination of out-side stimulation, review of accomplishments, and socializing. Where it is possi-ble, have a meeting at your home or other private setting. These important gestures add to the evidence that you take seriously both the task and the individuals.

Keep the board informed of committee progress and keep the committee informed of the board's responses. Communicate in personal ways with the committee between meetings. For example, if you've reported to the board, send a personal note so that they know the results of the presentation, includ-ing any actions taken. Too often we wait for the next committee meeting, when in fact the really interested members will be wondering, "What in the world happened to our important proposal?"

If there are newspaper stories or other bits of news that relate to the area of your committee's work, send them along with a note, "Thought this might be of interest." It's important to touch base with your own subordinates. What you should be aiming for is that some day, several years hence, you will bump into some of these people, and you want them to say, "You know, looking back on it, we really got some amazing things done. It was one of the most rewarding things I've ever done. And besides—it was fun."

For the committee member to earn a share in that ultimate reward, he or she also has to make an investment.

In the same Adult Education Association pamphlet, there is this very useful "Committee Member Check List":

1. Am I familiar with and sympathetic toward the aims and methods of the parent organization which created the committee?

2. Can I express myself easily and clearly and enjoy the give and take of exchanging ideas with others?

3. Do I have reasonably good focus, a sense of direction and a sense of timing, plus a willingness to stick to the task at hand?

4. Am I receptive, open minded and able to learn and to receive stimulation from others?

5. Do I have vision and perspective which enables me to see the present in terms of the future?

6. Am I fundamentally cooperative in seeking after agreement and unity?

7. Am I able to arrive at decisions and face their implications?

The "summary of specific responsibilities" says:

To be effective, committee members should be able to attend meetings regularly. They should seek to understand the Committee assignment and work to complete it. Members should participate in the deliberations and discussions and should share the responsibility of sticking to the subject and trying to understand and use the ideas of other members. They should help in reaching committee decisions, in committee action and in following the final disposition of its work. Committee members should also evaluate their own contributions to the Committee and share the responsibility for evaluating the work of the Committee as a whole.

If you are a board member serving on a committee with persons who are not on the board, accept responsibility to reach out to these people; they will be sensitive to how you as a board member relate to them. Help them understand the broader work of the organization and develop a sense of shared mission and pride. You can also help them realize limitations of the organization's resources, but don't constantly remind them that the board has many other priorities. Some board members can be insufferable in the way they exercise their membership on the board to stifle the initiative and growth of other committee members. Make it a rule to *really* listen to the others. Don't tell them you already covered that ground six years ago. Encourage and nurture them. They are the organization's seed crop. Besides, remember how you felt as a newcomer in some organization, and think hard about the people you remember as the best models of kindness and helpfulness. Someone helped bring you along, and now it's your turn.

At board meetings when your committee leader reports, be supportive. It's pretty unsettling and even maddening when a person makes a report, and the other committee members around the board table hedge their bets waiting to see how the other trustees react. It's your committee, too. Put yourself on the line.

Whether you are on the board or not, find ways to let the committee head know that you appreciate her or his leadership. You may not agree with everything being done and may even hold a different point of view on some subjects, but go out of your way to show your objectivity and thoughtfulness in giving thanks where they are due.

For all committee members, carry your share of the load. That may seem obvious, but it is the source of the greatest discouragement in all kinds of organizations. Depending on people who aren't reliable is a nightmare, and working with people who are is a delight.

For all the frustration and hard work, you will enjoy the satisfactions of the committee's accomplishments and the sense of personal worth. When the work is hard or dull or upsetting, try to remember the largest lesson I've ever learned about volunteering, which I tried to summarize in the opening chapter of this book:

> People who get involved with public causes open themselves to frustration and disappointment, but—through it all and after it all—those moments of making change happen for the better are among our lasting joys. There's something wonderfully rewarding in being part of an effort that makes a difference.

You may not feel that way at the end of tomorrow's committee meeting, but I bet you will five years from now.

11

Making the Most Out of Meetings

A significant part of the business of voluntary organizations involves meetings, and yet in most organizations surprisingly little thought is applied to making meetings productive. It is a fact of life that good meetings create high attendance, improve the quality of decisions, and promote alert follow-through. Bad meetings don't. Thoughtfulness and common sense are the basic ingredients of planning good meetings. These in turn lead to some rules that make up the art of having good meetings. I'll start with some suggestions that apply to both board and committee meetings and then turn to some special features of board and annual meetings.

Give careful attention to the selection, recruitment, and orientation of the group; these are the cornerstones of good meetings. Let me repeat my earlier advice to the presidents that it is important to select as the chairperson an individual who is an effective organizer rather than a person who is necessarily an authority on the subject at hand.

The group should have a sense of purpose. Some of this will come with orientation, but it should also be conveyed through the formal committee charge and in the reports from the president, chairperson, and others.

Spread the workload of the board or committee and of the meetings themselves. Try to be certain that several people are responsible for handling individual items on the agenda.

If you don't have topics that really need the group's consideration, cancel the meeting, even though the board or committee may not have missed a monthly meeting in 133 years.

Provide adequate notice and give a reminder call a day or two in advance of the meeting. If it's an ongoing body, have fixed meeting dates such as the first Monday of the month. If that's not possible, then it's generally helpful to have the group set its next meeting date while they are still in session; the day after the meeting, a notice should be sent reminding the full group of the next date or dates. It's helpful to enclose a return postcard so that you have an indication of attendance and the members feel they've made a firm commitment.

Send the agenda and the basic background material to the full group at least a week in advance of the meeting. I am constantly dismayed to find how often the agenda is distributed at the meeting, and even then it often consists of only three or four nondescript items such as "President's Report," "Executive's Report," and "New Business." If the members are worth involving, it's essential that they be served well. The greatest single factor in poor attendance is the failure to provide a good agenda and reference materials well in advance of the meeting. The agenda should state clearly what the group is being asked to consider or decide, and the reference material should prepare the members for intelligent discussion. If the people are committed to attend and if they see that the session is being organized in a business-like way, they're more likely to be there and at future meetings.

Pay careful attention to the physical arrangements, including location, accessibility, parking, and reasonable meal service. The room itself should be conducive to effective work, including good lighting, heat, and ventilation. If it is at all possible, I try to have a round table or a "square doughnut" so that all the members are facing the center. This creates maximum participation and a feeling of involvement for all. Even when I'm dealing with a board meeting of thirty to forty people, I try to organize it as a square donut or in two four-sided or three-sided tiers so that the group is fairly close together, all within earshot of one another and facing the center. Even with very large groups, I work hard at trying to create a physical arrangement that is comfortable and promotes maximum involvement. It's essential to plan in advance for blackboards, easels, and audiovisual equipment and to check electrical outlets, microphones, public address systems, and so on. Also, don't forget the arrangements for water and coffee service.

Check the meeting room well in advance. The day before the meeting, be certain that someone has the work order, knows you are coming, and knows what the arrangements are to be. Then check the meeting room one hour in advance of the meeting. I do this even with breakfast meetings. My experience is that 50 percent of the time, there is a breakdown in the arrangements. The blackboard will be there, but no chalk. There won't be an extension cord for the projector, or the electrical socket will be wired with the lights so that when the lights go out, the projector also goes out. Or the public address system won't work, or perhaps someone forgot to provide a microphone. And it happens at least 10 percent of the time that the meeting room isn't set up at all, and the only person around never heard of you or your damned meeting.

If your meeting is in a hotel, by all means check their bulletin board to see that the meeting time and place are clearly identified. I'll make a private bet with you that at least half the time the bell captain or the catering department have listed the wrong meeting room or the wrong time, and at least 25 percent of the time they will have forgotten to list you at all. It is always a matter of frustration to me that hotels that make so much of their money from meetings generally handle them so poorly. This is why it's essential to check doggedly on the arrangements a day in advance and in person an hour in advance.

Abide by Murphy's Laws:

- What can go wrong will go wrong.

- If unattended to, it will only get worse.

Don't let the chairperson or staff dominate the meeting. If either or both take up all the time, they may feel good at the end of the session, but they'll be talking to themselves at the next meeting.

Keep the group informed between meetings. This includes getting the minutes out quickly, reporting to the committee on action taken on their recommendations by the executive committee or board of directors, and sending thoughtful notes sharing interesting bits of information or news of the organization's activities. Whatever it is, a deliberate, thoughtful, ongoing effort to let the members know they are important and are appreciated will pay off.

Give the group a sense of accomplishment and momentum. The original charge to the group should have been realistic enough so that there can be a regular sense of accomplishment. If large tasks are broken down into bite-size pieces, the group can have a feeling of getting somewhere. Be sure that the members do gain a sense of movement and have the satisfaction of accomplishment. Committees and boards often suffer from a feeling of vagueness or vastness, and it takes considerable effort to provide the members with some feeling of tasks well done.

Keep it interesting. Deliberately plan part of the agenda for the purpose of giving the group a feeling of being in the know, having a chance to learn some of the exciting things that are happening in the field, or knowing more about what the organization as a whole is doing. I learned a lot from a president who insisted that every meeting should include a section that he labeled "the entertainment." It was his deliberate and successful policy that every meeting should include a film or speaker or some presentation to take the group away from the immediate tasks and give them a sense of excitement and being in the know.

Pay attention to the niceties. Take time to figure out how to make your meetings pleasant. For instance, people say how much they appreciate having large name cards placed in front of each person attending the meeting. Send the committee list with each agenda. Include first names and nicknames. This may seem like duplication, but people do forget names and like to review the list in advance.

Occasionally hold your meeting in a special setting. This doesn't mean it has to be in a fancy club. It might be in one of the facilities that relate to the group's efforts. The National Mental Health Association encourages local boards to meet at least once a year in a mental health facility serving the community.

Provide a regular mechanism for board acknowledgment of committee progress. This kind of thoughtfulness makes a big difference to committee members, who inevitably wonder if their efforts are really noticed and really do achieve results. Thank a committee when its work is done, and express appreciation to those who are going off the committee. It's hard to anticipate all the things that add up to the courtesies and to thoughtfulness, but unless presidents, committee chairpersons, and staff members take time to project themselves into the place of the members, the rush of everyday events will continue to preoccupy them, and important opportunities to develop a closer feeling of camaraderie and family will be lost.

All the basic rules apply to board meetings. In addition, there are special considerations. The board of directors has to have an overview of the mission, goals, progress, and problems of the agency, which means that a part of board meetings has to be given to this kind of review. It can be partly accomplished by a written report of the president, including a report of progress toward the annual agenda (the one-year plan).

One of the most important roles of the board is to establish the priorities and directions for the organization. This means that a reasonable amount of time must also be given to discussion and, when appropriate, to approval of the annual agenda, the annual budget, and the multi-year plan, and to regular determination of progress on those plans.

Because the board's decisions are so central to an agency's effectiveness, it is all the more necessary that the agenda and related material go out in advance. The board members should have an agenda in their hands at least a week in advance of the meeting. The supporting material should not be so voluminous that it will not be practical for board members to gain a grasp of the issues. This means that a good deal of work will have to be done by the president and executive director to reduce complicated issues to their essence. Some organizations throw in all the minutes of intervening committee meetings and then add insult to injury by having the chairperson read the minutes.

Don't expect that every board member is going to read everything, although if the material is distributed well beforehand, you'll be surprised at how many will. People who have a particular interest in a subject will carefully prepare for that discussion. The presentations and discussions should start with the assumption that people have read the material in advance of the meeting, and it should become an embarrassment for members to ask questions or make comments that clearly indicate they have not done their homework.

Carefully identify the reason for having each item on the agenda. Certain items will be there for important information purposes. Other items will be there for the board's consideration and disposition. One can't accurately predict which items will get fast action and which ones will require extensive debate. You may recall Parkinson's Law that the smaller the topic, the greater attention it will be given. He uses the example of the board that quickly passes on the purchase of a multimillion-dollar nuclear reactor and then gets hopelessly bogged down in a discussion of purchasing garbage cans. He says this is because everybody knows about garbage cans.

Provide a suggested timetable. This obviously will be adjusted to the board's pace, but at least it will provide some indication of the items that seem to require fuller consideration.

The board agenda and resource material should include intelligible financial reports—an income and expense statement, balance sheet, and budget status report.

Limit the executive director's report. For example, only occasionally do I make an extensive report to the board of directors. I consider that if my job is properly done, the reports of the various committees, task forces, and other officers will cover most of the business that needs attention. Occasionally I may want to share management considerations or special observations with the board. It's my impression that if I do not constantly dominate the board discussions, then the information and issues I *do* bring to the board will carry more weight. I shudder at the meetings I attend where the executive director and other staff members carry the ball so totally that the board members are left completely uninvolved, limp, and glassy-eyed.

Most membership organizations hold an annual meeting, which can and should be a special occasion. It's probably accurate to say that most annual meetings are dinner meetings and that by the time the group is finished with the meal, the reports, the elections, the outgoing president's comments, the incoming president's comments, the awards, and the responses of those honored with awards, those members still present are numb, disengaged, and dreading the main speech, which is still to come.

Annual meetings should be exciting and stimulating, and they should provide significant thrust for the organization's major business. For these reasons, the basic rules governing all meetings given in the first few pages of this chapter are particularly important. In addition, here are some other important considerations:

- **Treat the voting membership as an important part of your organization.** The annual meeting is an important time for the voting members to be involved and informed about your future plans.

- **Provide enough time for what needs to be done.** If you really line up all that can (and should) be done at the annual meeting, it is almost a certainty that it can't be reduced to a dinner meeting unless, as is too often the case, you are prepared to go well into the night. Instead, given enough advance notice, people will set aside a Saturday or a weekday or at least an afternoon topped by a really fun-filled and interesting dinner without all the business being crammed in. To do this: 1) adopt a time schedule and stick to it; 2) leave time for questions, discussion, and debate; and 3) provide an advance agenda with written reports. (Include written information on award winners, nominating committee recommendations, and summaries of the actions called for.)

- **Relate the meeting to the basic thrust of the association.** It's surprising how often organizations will choose themes and speakers that do not fit into or contribute to the mainstream of their current efforts. It's almost as though annual meeting committees were divorced from the basic organization. Often the pattern is to come up with a catchy theme and a principal speaker that do not take advantage of the tremendous opportunity to use the annual meeting as an occasion to advance the organization's basic projects.

- **Plan carefully for awards and recognition.** The annual meeting is a time when an organization can honor those who have served its cause. Be careful, though, not to present so many awards that the meaning is diminished. The awards can be listed in a printed program. In some cases, many people may be included in an award category—for instance, volunteers who have contributed more than 100 hours to the organization. These people can be asked to stand up as a group. If you are trapped into doing everything at a dinner meeting, present some of the awards in advance and then be sure the names are listed in the printed program. It's also effective sometimes to spread the awards throughout the agenda. Except in unusual cases, don't introduce individuals who aren't present. I always have a sinking feeling when names are called for people to stand and several of the people aren't present.

- **Select interesting locations.** It's not always possible to come up with an imaginative approach, but people do like to visit an interesting place. This can be either a new hotel or, at the other extreme, a facility that relates to the agency's work. Be careful about the expense, however. Increasingly, agencies are involving youth and people of all incomes and those $40 dinner tabs have a way of saying you don't really mean it. Consider, for a change, holding the meeting in a jail, state hospital, church, museum, campground, new synagogue, a mansion donated for the day, a community college, a movie theater or legitimate playhouse, city hall, a company's training facility, or any other place that's different, interesting, inexpensive, and perhaps educational.

- **Work hard at promoting attendance.** There should be early mailings to the voting membership and to a very carefully developed list of outside groups and individuals. A personal invitation should be extended by officers and members of the annual meeting committee to the fifty outside people you are most eager to have present. It should be made clear that the board members are expected to be there. Voting members should also know they are expected to attend this one meeting each year. Committee members are part of the voting membership, and they should be urged particularly to take advantage of this opportunity to get a broader feel of the organization. Promoting attendance requires imagination and hard work, but the annual meeting can be a very significant event in terms of public exposure, community involvement, and agency thrust. Some members of the annual meeting committee should carry on an extensive telephone campaign to the board members, voting members, committee members, and others to promote attendance.

- **Take advantage of your publicity opportunities.** Some of your promotion efforts can be assisted by advance notices to the news media. However, these will simply support your promotion efforts and should not be considered as doing the promotion job itself. The many events that will be part of a really good annual meeting will provide pegs for advance stories and for media coverage during the meeting itself.

- **Spread the workload.** One of the reasons that annual meetings often don't achieve their potential is that the event is left largely to the staff. However, it's the kind of activity at which many board members will work very hard. The annual meeting should be a major volunteer responsibility. The committee should be a year-round operation with regular reports to the board of directors.

The various assignments—involving publicity, registration, promotion, awards, and program—should be made to individuals or subcommittees. Obviously, staff backup is needed but not nearly so much as we generally think. Clearly, the opportunity and responsibility to make the most of this annual event should not be curtailed because staff members don't have enough time. Most of the responsibilities can be carried by volunteers.

- **Pay special attention to arrangements.** Remember, "What can go wrong, will go wrong." Make a careful list of all the physical arrangements and check them. If you don't, things will rapidly go wrong and Murphy's second law will come into play: "If unattended to the situation will only get worse."

Among the many things that can go wrong:

- the microphone or speaker system won't work (or will squeal so badly that people will think they're experiencing a lobotomy);
- the awards will be in the wrong order (or else they won't get there at all);
- the president will introduce the head table from left to right when it's set up right to left;
- the hotel will serve pot roast on Good Friday.

Don't be afraid of healthy controversy in meetings of committees, the board, or voting membership. If the cause is important, people will feel strongly about it but not always the same way. Let people debate and even argue, but keep it within the bounds and context of an organization's meeting. Don't be too quick to refer the issue to a committee or to try to mask very real differences. It amuses me when some well-meaning peacemaker will jump up and offer the observation that "they're really not that far apart," when the antagonists are at each other's throats, or "the two points are not mutually exclusive," when in fact the two arguments are opposite.

If the going gets too hot, fall back on *Robert's Rules of Order* to help organize the discussion and decision, but don't let that process take control of healthy exchange. (For a primer or review of some of the most commonly used

Robert's Rules, please see the first few pages of Appendix C—"Robert's Rules of Order Demystified").

Once the matter has been decided, the volunteer and staff leaders must help the organization adjust quickly to the decision and get on with the more positive aspects of the agency's program and operations. A good organization, like a good manager, spends time on issues that it can do something about and doesn't waste time on issues it can't do anything about.

Obviously, peacemaking should be the order of the day, but once in a while it's not the best course to follow. Occasionally, it's better that people lose and move out of the mainstream. There is a great temptation in voluntary organizations to make up and to bring Charlie back into the chairmanship or to the executive committee to show him there are no hard feelings. This is usually the right thing to do, but sometimes it only perpetuates the underlying difference that was finally settled. There are times—not often, to be sure, but there are times—when it's better to let some people fall away or go away mad. This may not seem fair—a contradiction to the kind of spirit that voluntary organizations try to generate—but some people and some controversies are better moved out so that the organization can concentrate on what the clear majority wants to do. Remember that an organization can sustain only so much controversy.

It is important to say a word about the annual meeting of national organizations. Much of what I said about annual meetings in general applies here, but the national annual meeting deserves special mention. It is the major vehicle by which national leaders can promote the spirit, thrust, camaraderie, and communication so necessary to the total organization. Often the board and even the national staff tend to take the annual meetings for granted. We don't realize the responsibility and opportunity it represents, and, thus, we don't set aside enough time to do it imaginatively and well.

As the executive director of the National Mental Health Association, I talked each year with the staff and meeting committee about the importance I attached to the national annual meeting. I described the kind of preparation I thought was necessary to make it an experience people would go away from with new respect for the association, new pride in the organization, and a storehouse of information to apply back home.

We went over our service plans to identify the problems and aspirations of our local units and to match people for meals and social functions in order to promote optimal communication and informal consultation. We set up our cocktail hours in a "cocktails and conversation" format so that people could go to specific tables or booths to talk about subjects of interest to them. This not only broke the ice—which is so essential to do—but it also provided people with a good deal of information and networking.

I'm sure it's the same with most national organizations, but the handbook governing all the technical arrangements for those annual meetings was a tome. It started with the selection of facilities and ran through a hundred pages or more, ending with instructions on providing tips to hotel employees who were particularly responsive. In between there was a collection of lessons learned that helped make certain that our meetings were professionally and thoughtfully done so that people went away with a confidence that their national association was well run and did care about them. This, in turn, instilled a greater spirit and commitment in our membership.

Not everyone can get to the national annual meeting, and we tend not to realize how helpful it is for people to see the organization beyond the limits of their own chapters. Some national organizations no longer have a national annual meeting. For instance, the Girl Scouts of America meet every three years. That organization uses the first of the intervening years for regional meetings, and the second for development and discussion of the issues that will be decided in the triennial national meeting. I favor some such system because regional or sectional meetings give many more people a feeling of being part of something bigger and special.

Whether you are responsible for a task force or international conference, work hard at producing good meetings. They are the key to good decision-making, all-out follow-through, and maximum volunteer motivation. It's on the meeting ground that the quality of the organization is truly revealed.

12

Fundraising

Almost every nonprofit organization needs money. This applies to fledgling organizations, groups in search of new sources of funds, United Way affiliated organizations that need to supplement their income through self-support, and many other organizations that need to raise money to support their existing programs or to expand.

Fundraising is hard work, but if you have a cause and program that deserve support and you're willing to work at it, you can raise money. Along the way, you and the organization will gain confidence, contacts, and camaraderie. One of the best expressions of all three comes from Booker T. Washington's experience in trying to raise money in the early days of the Tuskegee Institute. In the chapter on "Raising Money" from his book *Up From Slavery*, he says:

> While the work of going from door to door and from office to office is hard, disagreeable and costly in bodily strength, it has some compensations. Such work gives one a rare opportunity to study human nature. It also has its compensations in giving one an opportunity to meet some of the best people in the world—to be more correct, I think I should say *the best* people in the world. When one takes a broad survey of the country you will find that the most useful and

influential people in it are those that take the deepest interest in institutions that exist for the purpose of making the world better.

The fundraising commitment must begin with the board and must be high on the agenda of a significant number of the trustees. Not only must it be of high priority, it must also be high in status and recognition within the organization. That's not easy. If you're wondering how to get moving, you probably are familiar already with the problem of having board members not really recruited with fundraising responsibilities distinctly in mind. And if you're already getting most of your support from fees, contracts, or a federated fund such as United Way, it's even harder to stir up real fundraising interest and urgency. Raising money takes dogged persistence, bullheadedness, salesmanship, year-round cultivation, board support and encouragement, a plan, an attainable goal, and lots of excitement—to wit, it's hard work. But if the board decides it is going to raise money and is willing to allocate at least 20 percent of its energy and resources to accomplish it, you can and will succeed.

It's fascinating to hear people today speak about the American Heart Association's success. They assume that the organization couldn't help but succeed. They will go on at great length about how the organization had a visible cause, leadership, fundraising staff, dollars to invest, and a basic fundraising blueprint; how the total association was organized and dedicated primarily to raising funds; and how, in the early 1950s, there was a wide-open climate for fundraising.

Fifty years ago the real picture was similar to that of most organizations today that are trying to figure out how to raise money. There wasn't a visible cause; heart attack victims looked so normal that there was no chance to get the kind of sympathy one could generate with a poster showing a child polio victim. We didn't have leadership; certainly we didn't have the community leaders with us. Most of the leaders were physicians, who took little interest in fundraising. We didn't have a fundraising staff—most of us were young idealists with far more fire than knowledge. We didn't have very many dollars, certainly not the kind of money necessary to prime the pump of a major campaign. We didn't have a blueprint for campaigning; indeed, we were floundering around trying to figure out whether to develop and sell valentines or go into the United Fund, raise money by mail, or accept government grants. And the organization certainly didn't have a fundraising determination. In terms of fundraising climate, everywhere we went we were told that people were tired of volunteering and fed up with being asked to contribute, and that we should look to the Community Chest for support. It was terribly difficult to get local groups interested in fundraising and convinced that they could do it.

In fifty years the American Heart Association has gone from that beginning to an annual income approximating $500 million!

What evolved during the 1950s was, first, that local boards were convinced that money had to be raised; then gradually came the recruitment of campaign chairs who were willing to join up and give it a try, and a growing pervasive spirit for making each February's totals better than the February before.

As often happens, the darkest days turned out to provide some very real blessings. Throughout the 1950s and 1960s, the American Heart Association was fighting to survive United Way's determination to take the association in or else to dry up its income sources. We lost a good many chapters, and we lost a great many board members. Indeed, we seemed to lose most of the bigger names we had tried so hard to recruit. It turned out, however, that those who stayed with us were a hardy lot. Contrary to belief, they were not often the significant community leaders. They were independent souls who were not frightened away and, by standing up and being counted, brought a verve, backbone, and determination to the agency that has been its true making.

The American Heart Association has grown rapidly, expanding its income and its sources of funds. Its 2001 income profile looked like this:

Income Source	
Contributions	$114,361,228
Contributed Materials	6,350,403
Contributed Services	10,201,070
Net Special Events	165,468,374
Bequests	82,912,024
Split-Interest Agreements	15,093,231
Fund-Raising Agencies	21,386,784
Other Income*	94,158,461
Grand Total	**$509,931,575**

*Other income includes program fees, sales of educational materials, membership dues, investment income, and royalty revenue.

I often think of those early years, particularly when I hear all the same reasons why it can't be done today, and when I'm asked if I think an organization can raise money for general support or for a new program or affiliate.

Every time I'm asked by a board delegation if I think their organization can raise money, I repeat that they are in for some awfully hard work. I don't say this to discourage them. Indeed, I hope they'll push on, and I hope this applies to you. But if you're timid, or your organization isn't really determined, you won't survive the obstacles, heartaches, and difficulties that, unfortunately, I can promise you are ahead. On the other hand, if you have a cause that deserves support and you're willing to scratch, kick, and beg, you *can* raise money.

The procedure for getting a new or renewed fundraising effort under way should be something like this:

- **Convince your fellow trustees to make a full commitment.** I'll come back later to the board's fuller role.

- **Define the need.** This doesn't have to be an elaborate brochure, but define why you need money and try to come up with a needs goal. This shouldn't be "pie in the sky," but it shouldn't be too timid, either. What does your group really think it actually needs as a minimum to make a significant difference in the next three years?

- **Develop a fundraising plan.** Basically, a plan involves the following:

  a. *Identify the type or types of fundraising to be undertaken.* On the basis of consultation with other agencies, persons who have been involved in fundraising in the community, and consultants available to you from a parent organization, you will begin to get an idea of where your immediate potential rests. Don't scatter your shots too widely, but, as they say, don't put all your "begs in one ask-it" either. Later in this chapter, I'll talk about the various fundraising categories you can consider.

  b. *Establish a realistic goal for the first year.* Don't shoot immediately for your needs goal unless you have an angel or two in the wings or unless your needs are very modest. Set a goal that is attainable based on the sources of funds and the number of campaign workers it is going to be possible to recruit. Start small. Most campaigns tend to fall apart because the initial efforts are so ambitious as to be beyond the capacity of the organization. If a group becomes discouraged the whole effort quickly falls apart. On the other hand, if you set an attainable goal (and I don't mean that it has to be unduly modest) and you hit it, the organization will, in spirit and in fact, be on its way.

c. *Determine exactly how many board members and other campaign workers you need to make the contacts necessary to raise that amount of money.* Here, too, be realistic. Determine the deployment of these campaign workers in terms of teams and the consequent need for captains and other leaders. Make the jobs bite-size. Campaigns easily fall apart because unrealistic burdens are placed on too few people who either won't accept the jobs or don't follow through.

d. *Set a firm timetable for recruitment, training, campaigning, reporting, and recognition.* It will be terribly important to provide enough time. This doesn't mean that things can't be pulled together in a hurry, but if you're unreasonable, you just won't have time to do the job.

e. *Decide on the budget.* It needn't cost an arm and a leg, but the campaign is going to cost some money, and you have to be prepared to budget for the operation. If the budget won't cover what you're trying to do, you may be able to get some seed money from a corporation, foundation, or individual. More on this later.

- **Bring the plan back to the full board to get their firm support.** This includes approval of the budget, dollar commitments of support from individual board members, and guarantees of service. You may find at this point that some of the board members fall away, and you'll need to adjust your plans accordingly. Even though it's discouraging, it's better to have some shaking out at this point so that those remaining are as committed as you to get the job done.

- **Recruit the chairperson.** This is the most critical step. He or she needn't come from within the organization but should be someone who has a demonstrated capacity to accomplish the plan. Beware of talkers and, above all, don't seek a fast sell. This is one of the most important recruitment jobs you'll ever do.

- **Establish and keep to a regular schedule of training sessions and report meetings.**

- **Provide for recognition and awards.**

- **Put some of your best campaign volunteers on the board.**

- **Develop your second-year plan, with heavy involvement of those who participated in the first success.**

This all sounds very pat, and I certainly don't mean to suggest that if one is willing to follow these steps, success is automatic. However, there's a much better chance of getting there if this kind of proven pattern is followed.

Right from the start you'll wonder where you're going to find the volunteers to carry on the campaign. The answer is that your volunteers are out there, but you've got to work hard to find them. People want a cause and are willing to join up if you can only reach them.

What I said earlier about cold canvassing to recruit new board members applies here too. Many times I've gone into a community absolutely cold and have succeeded in recruiting a campaign chairperson. My pattern is to go to priests, ministers, rabbis, the mayor, the head of a service club, heads of women's groups, and persons who have worked in other campaigns. I ask them if they can identify people who may wish to take on the kind of job I have outlined, and it is rare that this pattern does not produce a chairperson. Each prospect I talk to who says no, I ask to be willing to help the chairperson who is finally recruited, so that even if I get several turndowns, my chances are improved because I've got a growing cadre of helpers already lined up.

You've got to look to your board of directors for help, but through sad experience I know that if someone on the board has not already come forward, the situation is not likely to change. However, go over the list carefully to be sure that many of them are at least lined up to help.

Actually, the chairperson will be the kind who can do a good deal of her or his own recruiting, but don't leave your recruit all alone and out on a limb. He or she can give only so much time and because each chairperson is only one person, if you're going to make as large a step as possible in the first year, you're going to need a lot of helpers. Look to people who have been helped by the organization or who have shown some interest in the cause. If the jobs are indeed bite-size, more people will be willing to help and will produce.

One of the greatest problems with fundraising and within nonprofit organizations generally is the confusion between the fundraising roles for board and staff. In terms of accountability, it is a board function, and it's a rare situation that the function can be delegated substantially to staff members. Sometimes, if it's entirely a direct-mail effort, a specialized staff working with highly sophisticated mail houses can handle it all. More often the campaign depends on recruitment of people with good contacts, and it's not realistic or reasonable to expect staff members to have enough of these connections.

The campaign, therefore, is almost always a board function. It can be delegated to a board committee consisting of board members and others, with staffing by the chief staff officer, or, if the position exists, the fundraising director. All trustees should be expected to contribute and to raise funds within their means and contacts. The committee should be responsible to the board. If the head of the committee or drive is not a member of the board, he or she should be invited to all board meetings, even when the agenda does not call for discussion of campaign progress. Most agendas should include the topic.

One of the most inappropriate things a board can do is to call for increased income and leave it to the staff to produce; or to recruit the head of the drive and then turn back to the "real" work of the organization, which usually involves planning for expending funds that the poor bloke isn't going to raise—not your way anyway.

The board is accountable—and the board leads. If it can't contribute or raise the funds, it must put together a campaign committee that can do the job and then back that group with every dollar, hour, and huzzah it can muster.

If your reaction, and maybe even the staff's, is to apologize for becoming too much like a fundraising organization—and maybe even to decline too much involvement because "we're essentially a program agency" or because "I'm here because I'm a program person"—cancel the campaign until and unless the tune is changed to "I know how important it is to raise money, so how can I help?"

If your cause *really* needs the money, but too many board members won't help, plan for turnover. If you think that's going too far, you turn over.

Over the years, including times of economic downturn and government cutbacks in support for the programs and services of voluntary organizations, I've met with at least two hundred board and staff delegations seeking advice on development. I start with the same encouragement I give in this chapter, but I also follow up quickly with how much work is in store. I indicate that their organization must be prepared to devote at least 20 percent of its resources to fundraising and that the board and chief staff officer will have to devote closer to one-third of their time for the first few years. Despite their apparent conviction, the reaction is rarely, "If that's what it's going to take, we'll do it!" In the majority of cases, the reaction is rejection, anger, and insult.

Often the chief staff officer is the most offended. Those physicians, social workers, historians, or former foreign service officers are deeply upset that I should undercut their professional status by putting them in such a substantial fundraising role. I always try to convey that fundraising is really a matter of the people who care about a cause and know it firsthand, telling the story with the same conviction that they tell it every day to colleagues, friends, and neighbors.

Most of these delegations leave shaking their heads, already thinking about finding more reasonable advice. Later, I hear that they have merged, reduced their focus substantially, closed, or are looking for a new executive director. I can predict that in the interim, they went into further deficit or secured a grant from a foundation or board member to hire a development director to whom they turned over the noxious assignment.

I know I'm being uncharacteristically direct here, but it's deliberate. My primary message is to tell you how much you can do and to urge you to proceed with optimism. However, that would be irresponsible if I didn't couple it with the truest lessons I've ever learned in community organizing, all involving what it takes to launch and sustain a significant fundraising effort.

I mentioned the process of hiring a development director. Institutions are often willing to pay about anything for an experienced fundraising executive. That's often because boards and executive directors are willing to do almost anything to get someone else to perform their jobs. The good development directors are worth what they are being paid, but those very same specialists are good in large part because they know—and will tell you—that they can succeed only to the extent that the board and staff leadership are committed to and involved in the fundraising. It will not work for the board to assign the task to the executive director, and it will not work for the executive director to pass it on to the fundraising director. On the other hand, if all three work together as a team, the results can be terrific.

For the board member in a smaller organization, I've no doubt belabored quite enough the matter of experienced fundraising executives. Let me acknowledge quickly that most campaigns don't require a full-time trained fundraiser. Many groups find someone who can devote a realistic amount of time to the job. I advise these groups to look to effective women or retired persons who may not want full-time employment. You'll be surprised how much experience and ability are already out there in the community. Talk to other agency volunteers and staff, your United Way, and community leaders who have been identified with major causes—they may be able to lead you to the right person.

Generally, I advise small and mid-size associations not to engage fundraising firms to serve as staff for ongoing community campaigns. Many of these groups are expert in planning and conducting capital gifts campaigns, and specialty firms and specialty departments of the larger firms are often skilled in direct-mail solicitation, bequest cultivation, church "every-member" drives, special events, and many other fundraising categories. As such, they raise a great deal of money for voluntary organizations. I have tremendous respect for the ability of fundraising firms, notably those associated with the American Association of Fund-Raising Counsel (AAFRC). The only fundraising role I've generally found them not particularly suited for is staffing the annual community campaigns of such groups as voluntary health agencies. Many of the fundraising firms with which I've worked are the first to point out that they are not organized to provide this service. Their experience and professionalism make them more expensive than most local groups can afford on a regular basis, and most local voluntary agencies don't have at hand or in early prospect sufficient community leadership to raise the sums that would justify the fees these firms have to charge.

I generally discourage groups from hiring a person whose full-time job is working part-time for several agencies (except in the area of special events, where many experts routinely help several different organizations). In my experience this arrangement rarely works well.

Build into your three-year campaign plan a firm estimate of staff needs, and make the switch as soon as you can go to your own full-time person. This may be hard on the individual whose part-time efforts have brought you to that happy transition, but if you're going to grow and sustain the momentum, you will need an individual who is good and is employed full-time.

I know I seem to be preoccupied with the staffed operation, and many of you are ready to burst with exclamations of how much your organization already raises without staff. My rule of thumb is that if a campaign is going to involve several fundraising categories and an annual goal of more than $100,000, some backup is usually needed. However, many organizations prove the exception.

Many organizations have board members who have more experience and savvy than most staff people, and those fundraising efforts are models of high yield and low cost. The basic rule is for the board to do everything possible on its own and to hire staff only when that will help the volunteers reach even higher results.

Let me turn to various categories of fundraising, beginning with a quick look at where the country's contributions come from.

In 2001, according to *Giving U.S.A.,* published by the AAFRC Trust for Philanthropy, Americans gave $210 billion to close to a million nonprofit institutions and agencies. Seventy-six percent came from living individuals. As indicated earlier, 89 percent of all American adults make contributions to the causes of their choice. This clearly represents good news for you because it tells you that you probably have potential among the broadest possible pool of citizens in your community.

The next most important sources of support in 2001 were foundations at 12 percent, bequests at 8 percent, and corporations at 4 percent. (It should be noted that the 4 percent for corporate contributions is only the amount that businesses claim under the contributions category of their tax returns. Most businesses, particularly mid-size and smaller ones, simply report their contributions as business expenses. The total contributed, therefore, would far exceed the 4 percent, probably at least doubling.)

Because individual causes and organizations differ so much, all I can do is present some of the fundraising categories so that you can get a feel for the possibilities. It will be important to work closely with experienced individuals and groups in the development of your own campaign plan, including the specific categories that you desire to pursue.

1. **Special gifts.** This is a pretty sophisticated kind of fundraising; it's been my experience, however, that you can often go to well-to-do people or to foundations or corporations with a specific plea for leadership gifts or start-up grants. I've seen a number of organizations go to ten or fifteen such sources and ask for $500 or $5,000 a year from each for two years as a means of getting this kind of campaign started. This of course means that you are going to have to replace this money with new gifts at the end of two years, but that is part of your gamble and commitment. When we started INDEPENDENT SECTOR, we turned to a number of foundations and business corporations for start-up assistance. With most, we asked for $30,000, with $15,000 for the first year, $10,000 for the second, and $5,000 for the third. We guaranteed that everything possible would be done to replace that "soft" or temporary money with "hard" dues from a growing number of members. During that first three years, the board spent a good deal of its time, and I devoted at least one-third of mine, to membership development and other fundraising efforts. When the grants ran out, the core budget was carried by dues income.

   Beyond leadership or start-up gifts, you may well find that there are upper-income families who may surprise you by having quite an interest in your cause. Carefully develop your list, and be certain that these people are seen personally. There will be a great temptation to say that a personalized letter going to 500 such people is better than trying to see ten or fifteen personally, but don't believe it.

   Your campaign plan can include a growing list of such personal contacts each year so that at the end of five years you will have a fairly sophisticated special gifts campaign launched.

2. **Community and family foundations.** An experienced executive of an older organization or a bank trust officer can quickly identify the likely community and family foundations. These should be approached for leadership gifts or start-up/expansion grants, although some may be willing to provide an annual gift for several years, and others may be willing to make at least a small contribution. Don't be timid—go to see them and tell your story. Your

heart may be pounding, and your hands may be shaking, but your conviction will come through, and that is often what tips the scales.

Obviously, if a member of your board or campaign organization knows some of the individuals involved, this assistance should be used to its fullest extent—both as a door opener and to help sell the cause. In these categories, don't assume that someone won't give. Remember the story of Vivian Beaumont, who gave one of the major buildings that now stands in the Lincoln Center complex in New York. With dismay, one of her friends asked her why she had given her money to Lincoln Center and not to another theater with which she and the friend were identified, and Vivian Beaumont's surprised reply was, "Because they asked me!"

3. **Door-to-door solicitation.** Door-to-door campaigns are still one of the means of raising substantial sums of money. You don't have to organize the whole community or region, you can start with certain neighborhoods. If I had to go from point zero to the maximum dollars in the shortest possible time, I would still use the door-to-door campaign as the heart of my effort.

    You can generally find people who have had experience with this kind of campaign who are willing to advise you—if not assist you—and they can often lead you to someone who will take on the task. Don't get too ambitious the first year—you'll begin to have dollar signs in your eyes when you think of the potential of reaching every house and when you hear what the American Cancer Society is raising by this method. If you are too ambitious to start with, the operation will collapse, and it will be all the harder next year. Decide what part of the community you can realistically tackle the first year, and be satisfied to bite off just that much, with the assurance that there will be other years.

4. **Businesses.** Business giving is a growing side of philanthropy, and an increasing number of corporations try to assist with more than just cash, as important as that is. They donate equipment, provide for printing, contribute furniture, give low-interest or no-interest loans ("program-related investments"), encourage

participation of their employees, and in many other ways help in the maintenance and development of community and national organizations. Alex Plinio, then president of the Prudential Foundation, started out to write a paper entitled "Twelve Ways That Companies Help Voluntary Organizations with Other Than Cash Contributions." Each time he presented the paper, someone mentioned types of giving that he had left out. He finally ended with something like "Forty-One Ways . . . ." The paper by Plinio and co-author JoAnne Scanlan was published by INDEPENDENT SECTOR with the title "Resource Raising: The Role of Non-Cash Assistance in Corporate Philanthropy."

5. **Labor groups.** Don't overlook the labor organizations. They have a history of significant generosity to worthwhile causes and may be quite sympathetic about helping a struggling new organization or launching a new effort by an existing organization.

6. **Special events.** Special events are probably the most ubiquitous of America's fundraising efforts. Special events are going on almost all the time and almost everywhere. These events include balls, auctions, bake sales, golf tournaments, walk-a-thons—an almost endless list of projects.

   My own approach is usually to get clubs and organizations to put on special events for the cause. It's better to have many organizations putting on special events than to have your association trying to develop events. All this generates considerable publicity and attention, which can lead to gifts from the treasuries of the various organizations and to some volunteers from them.

   Special events may well have a prominent place in your initial campaign plan as one of the fastest means of making some money. I'm inclined to caution you, however, about major dependence on only one special event. In the long run, they have a way of wearing out and ending up a somewhat fickle source of ongoing support. There are, of course, magnificent exceptions, but generally these are rarities and any one special event is not a secure way of funding an ongoing operation.

7. **Testimonials.** Many organizations use the testimonial approach. Some organizations raise a great deal of money this way and are able to sustain the operation. Most organizations, however, find it a means of raising immediate money for a special situation without the expectation that like sums can be generated each year.

   The approach is to identify an individual who is esteemed and who deserves the honor. It's also necessary to pick someone who is sufficiently revered, feared, or central to people's economy that they will be willing to pay $100 or much more to honor him or her. These testimonials are usually dinners, and the emphasis is on selling tables to organizations, business associates, and others who are eager to participate in the testimonial.

8. **Retail sales.** Many organizations raise money through the sale of cookies, apple butter, flowers, magazines, aprons, Christmas cards, and myriad other objects. This can be an expensive proposition, so go into it with your eyes open. Many commercial groups will actively enlist your participation in selling their products, with a part of the profit going to your organization. Some of these arrangements can be very helpful to organizations, but generally they are primarily helpful to the companies promoting the idea.

9. **Media appeals.** Unfortunately, direct appeals for money through public media announcements have pretty much worn themselves out. Very little money is raised this way except for emergency or unusually dramatic appeals. It's almost certain that someone in your organization will suggest that this is the solution to your troubles, but I warn you that, although it will provide useful publicity, it probably will not provide significant income.

10. **Direct mail.** Direct mail has proven to be a very useful source of income for many organizations. A direct-mail approach usually requires a cause that has a broad appeal, but specialists can help zero in on an audience that fits your profile. This effort requires a very sophisticated, professional direct-mail specialist. You'll need money to have a field test done, and then if the field test is successful, you'll still have to expect the first year to come close to a washout with expenses equaling income. If renewal rates hold up

for the second and third years, the net income for the cause can be substantial.

Direct mail tried through your own office to a wide constituency will not usually pay for itself. Many organizations have to discover this for themselves. It seems so natural that with a cause as stirring as you believe yours to be, people are bound to respond to a heartrending letter. It just doesn't happen that way.

11. **Memorials and honorary gifts.** Many organizations have successfully promoted memorial and honorary gifts. The American Heart Association has probably been the most successful in the area of memorial gifts. This falls naturally in their direction because of the unfortunately high proportion of deaths caused by heart disease. In 2001, memorial gifts constituted approximately $25 million of the American Heart Association's income. If you're not in a death-related cause, however, memorials are not a likely source of substantial income. You may want to cite the success stories of some churches and synagogues, but I submit that their successes are also grounded in their unique relationship to death.

However, honorary gifts have been successfully promoted by many organizations. This takes very careful and long-term cultivation. It involves creating a habit among your own members and gradually among a widening circle of friends so that they automatically think of the honorary gift as a way of expressing special congratulations to people on the occasion of a birthday, baptism, marriage, bar mitzvah, anniversary, Easter, or other holiday.

A growing number of people send a simple postcard at Christmas indicating that, in lieu of many Christmas gifts, they have made one donation in the name of their friends to a particular charity.

12. **Membership.** Memberships represent a slow but very secure long-term source of support. In many campaign plans I've developed, such support starts low and rises steadily, while the special events category starts high but doesn't increase substantially. Membership dues should be at a high enough dollar amount to provide for regular service of the members and support for the programs. A minimum of $25 is wise, and I would usually go for

$50 or more. Members should be recruited from the board. Every board member should be at least a contributing member, if not a special giver. Then move to past board members, current committee members, the persons served by the agency, and those persons who have shown an interest in the cause. Watch the circles expand. As many potential members as possible should be approached personally. Until you have a chance to recruit a very wide group personally, you may want to approach some of the more likely prospects by phone or mail. Some organizations have been successful in setting up membership booths at conventions and meetings of other groups.

Set a specific goal in terms of the eventual proportion of the population you want to enlist as members. For instance, a local mental health association strives to enlist and hold a minimum of one-half of one percent of the population. This gives an organization something very specific to shoot at, and the goal can be divided into annual targets.

13. **Bequests.** A fast growing source of donated funds is bequests. Bequests now constitute approximately 8 percent of American giving, or about $16 billion. Bequest cultivation is a very sophisticated form of fundraising and obviously cannot be counted in your short-term fundraising plans. For organizations that are building long-term fundraising projects, however, a realistic proportion of the effort should be reserved for bequest cultivation.

Several years ago I was able to bring an unusual group together to provide guidelines for what I wanted to be a very serious and successful bequest promotion for a local chapter of the American Heart Association. The group was assembled by the chief judge of the probate court and included other probate judges, trust officers of major financial institutions, and tax and estate lawyers. All were assured that they would not have direct fundraising responsibility, but would only provide a blueprint for the organization to follow. As so often happens when a group gets involved and interested, we were able to recruit successfully several of the individuals (obviously not including the judges) to lead the implementation.

In a series of three meetings chaired by the chief judge, the group produced the following blueprint, which was followed and very shortly began to provide substantial legacies. In the intervening years, the program has produced almost staggering results with surprisingly little effort.

1. **Basic Assumptions**

   a. That a very small proportion of the Bar writes 75 percent of the wills that include gifts to charity.
   b. That these lawyers are almost always community figures or seen by their clients as important in the community.
   c. That most people who have money to leave are not certain which charities to consider.
   d. That lawyers who are community leaders are frequently asked by will-writing clients to suggest examples of worthy charities or asked if certain causes are really okay.
   e. That a bequest cultivation program is not as long-range as might be assumed because most people write or amend wills when there is reason to be concerned.
   f. That lawyers are interested in and curious about heart disease.
   g. That broad-scale mail campaigns with fancy brochures don't really make a dent.

2. **The Program That Evolved**

   a. We used several members of the original group to form our bequest cultivation committee.
   b. The committee screened the names of the will-writing attorneys. (I learned that these can be pretty quickly identified by checking which lawyers in your community are members of the two relevant American Bar Association sections dealing with taxation and estates.)
   c. It turned out that there were about 170 such attorneys in a metropolitan area of approximately two million. We expanded our committee to include several more of the 170.
   d. We held several meetings of the committee to help explain the problems of heart disease and the work of the American Heart Association.
   e. Our basic approach was for every committee member to "adopt" twelve fellow will-writing attorneys. The assignment included:

1) An initial luncheon or evening session. These were usually held at the committee member's club or home with the purpose of outlining: where we stand in heart disease control, how an individual can protect himself/herself, what the American Heart Association is, and a plan for future mailings.

2) Once every year thereafter, the committee member sent a personal letter to the attorneys for whom he or she was responsible. The mailings included the current annual report and other progress reports.

3) The object was not to hard sell but rather to be certain that the 170 will-writing attorneys were given a chance to know more about heart disease and the American Heart Association.

f. One of the basic steps the committee recommended was that every member of the board of directors of the association should include a bequest, however small, in his or her will.

Even this long list of campaign categories doesn't begin to cover all the possibilities, but it will give you some feel for the most likely things to be explored. I have not included any discussion of such devices as gift annuities, gifts of appreciated property, charitable remainder trusts, and many other important sources of funds. These will generally not be applicable until you have built a corps of annual givers and committed supporters. (For more detail about these and other categories, you may want to secure another Foundation Center book, *Securing Your Organization's Future: A Complete Guide to Fundraising Strategies* by Michael Seltzer.)

Don't try to tackle too many sources at once. When you finally decide which ones fit your organization, go after them with ferocious determination, and you'll find that the dollars will begin to multiply.

Fundraising doesn't have to cost much money, but raising money does involve certain costs. Most of the costs are the staff time applied to the fundraising operation. Usually only the very small campaigns or the very large campaigns can keep costs below 10 percent; the middle area becomes more expensive. Indeed, if you need staff assistance but are not at the point of attracting large gifts, the cost of the operation will almost have to be greater than 10 percent. This isn't unethical and shouldn't shock or deter anybody. My own gut reaction is that an ongoing campaign is ethical and justified if its costs are one-third or less. If this means that your agency is able to raise a lot more money than it otherwise would, which results in greater pursuit of its public mission, most givers will accept the morality and logic of that.

Some initial campaigns will cost even more than 30 percent. Direct-mail campaigns usually break even the first year, but if the field tests safely project that by the third year your renewals will be at a level that your costs are down to the one-third level, I'd encourage you to go ahead. I've been involved in initial community campaigns that cost more than 50 percent. It bothered me, but on the other hand I knew that this was necessary to get the operation going, and I knew that subsequent years' costs would drop to well below one-third.

In some campaigns involving sales of goods, the costs may routinely run above 50 percent. This is all right as long as the givers are satisfied that they are simultaneously getting something they want and helping a cause. It's not fair if people are pressured into taking something they don't want or if the impression is left that most of the money will be going to charity. In some sales efforts, however, most of the money does go to charity, particularly if the sales items are donated.

If you would like to know more about specific fundraising standards that have been developed by a knowledgeable group, please see Appendix B, "Standards for Charitable Accountability of the BBB Wise Giving Alliance."

An annual campaign provides impetus for telling the association's story, which is almost always very healthy for the organization. Even if it's only a membership effort conducted by an agency involved in the United Way, it's an opportunity to remind a growing number of people who you are, what you represent, what you can do for them, and what they can do for you.

Fundraising campaigns can be fun. They are almost always exciting. They provide a rallying point for the organization and in many ways lend an air of excitement to the whole operation. They're also hard work! And sustaining the effort year in and year out is particularly tough. You'll need to carefully and quickly promote volunteers up through the campaign organization (and surely from the campaign organization to the board), so there can be new blood and fresh leadership moving forward to share in the excitement of the campaign and thus be stimulated to carry the burdens of it.

One of the basic responsibilities of the campaign chairperson is to help recruit a replacement. This is also one of the president's responsibilities. Place the responsibility firmly with one of them, but make it clear that the other has got to stand ready to help and to see that it happens.

You must constantly seek ways to make clear to the workers how much their efforts mean. When I was director of the American Heart Association in Baltimore, every year we sent a New Year's card to each of the 7,000 or more block workers with a message something like: *"During the Season of Good Will, we want to thank you again for your wonderful service to your community as a Heart Association Volunteer."*

Successful fundraising performance has to be acknowledged and applauded throughout the organization. Find every possible way to say "thank you" and to give people the good feeling of accomplishment to which they are entitled. People want a cause. You have to help your people realize that they've got a good one, and not only is the association doing great things, but it is also grateful for the campaign volunteers' efforts. If you've achieved your goal, save a lot of the praise for the board too.

13

Budgeting and Financial Accountability

By their very nature, voluntary associations operate with public support and, therefore, have a responsibility to spend their money judiciously and to report on their expenditures to the public. In the earlier chapter on the role of board members I emphasized that, "Whether as board members you are called trustees, directors, governors, or something else, you are in essence the trustees in the literal and legal sense of the term. No matter how the organization is structured or the degree of authority delegated to staff, committees, or affiliates, the board and therefore the trustees are ultimately accountable." In the BoardSource booklet *Financial Responsibility of the Nonprofit Board*, author Andrew S. Lang says:

> Board members must understand the issues important to financial integrity and solvency, safeguards and procedures to protect the organization, and signs of financial trouble. Armed with this knowledge, they will be able to protect and enhance the nonprofit organization's capacity to serve the community.

An organization that handles more than $100,000 should have an independent audit and, therefore, is bound by the accounting practices spelled out in the various audit guides published by the American Institute of Certified Public Accountants (AICPA). For instance, their audit guide *Not-for-Profit Organizations—Audit and Accounting Guide* (2002) describes red flags that auditors should look for "to evaluate whether there is substantial doubt about the client's ability to continue as a going concern," such as:

- Insufficient unrestricted revenues to provide supporting services to activities funded by restricted contributions.

- A high ratio of fundraising expenses to contributions received or a low ratio of program expenses to total expenses.

- Insufficient resources to meet donor's restrictions. (This may result from the use of restricted net assets for purposes that do not satisfy the donor's restrictions, sometimes referred to as interfund borrowing.)

- Activities that could jeopardize the organization's tax-exempt status and thus endanger current contribution levels.

- Concern expressed by governmental authorities regarding alleged violations of state laws governing an organization's maintenance or preservation of certain assets, such as collection items.

- A loss of key governing board members or volunteers.

- External events that could affect donors' motivations to continue to contribute.

- Decreases in revenues contributed by repeat donors.

- A loss of major funding sources.

A companion piece to the AICPA guide is the *Standards of Accounting and Financial Reporting for Voluntary Health and Welfare Organizations* published by and available from the National Assembly of National Voluntary Health and Social Welfare Organizations, National Health Council, and United Way of America. According to the Standards foreword, "Adoption and use of the standards presented in this publication will enable voluntary health and welfare organizations to report their income and expenditures uniformly and in terms the contributing public can understand."

Even if your organization is not required to have an audit, you should consult an auditor to determine what requirements or practices are necessary to protect board members, the organization, and the public, and to help structure your accounting system and your basic financial reports, including the budget, income and expense statement, and balance sheet. They will also advise you on what reports you are required to submit to state and federal authorities and the timetable for them.

In this chapter I will assume that your operation is sufficiently large to be audited and that there is probably a need to delineate the separate roles of the board and staff, beginning with the budget.

Without getting into an exhaustive review of budget-making, it might be useful to comment briefly on the process of developing income and expense projections. Usually, leaders of voluntary operations are so close to the cause, or so overwhelmed with how much needs to be done, that they will overestimate income and underestimate expenses. The hard-headed realism of the treasurer and the finance committee is essential as an offsetting influence.

Income projections should be based on a practical and objective analysis of current sources of income, including a source-by-source and gift-by-gift review. This not only makes for practical budgeting but also provides sensible preparation for the degree of work necessary to renew gifts and grants and find new money. It's essential not to budget substantial new income—certainly not to count on it, to cover fixed expenses. The usual approach for nonprofit agencies is to hope so desperately for new income that it's counted in the budget; then, when it doesn't materialize, the agency ends up with a deficit or horrendous cutback. The wiser approach is to have an opportunity for budget revision during the year to allow additions according to new income actually produced.

If you have staff, expense projections are usually developed by the staff director. Here the volunteer president should be carefully consulted, and, of course, the treasurer and finance committee will be closely involved.

It is important that the finance committee never be allowed the authority to make decisions that rightfully belong to the executive committee or board. Many finance committees, in their efforts to cut or control expenditures, will make decisions about what activities should stay or go, which is beyond their authority. They should say to the president, staff, and board that their appraisal of income projections will not sustain the expenses budgeted. Then, if the board agrees with the finance committee's figures, it is up to the board and staff to decide where the cuts will be made.

The budget should be prepared early enough so that the full board of directors can be involved in its review and approval before the beginning of the fiscal year.

The format for the budget should include at least:

- A narrative summary of the year ending and the year ahead;

- A five-year review of income and expenses;

- A proposed budget including, for each line item, the prior year's budget, the prior year's actual expenditures and income, and the recommended allocations for the coming year.

You will note that a narrative summary is recommended. I worked with one treasurer for six years, and we had a perfect relationship, except once a year we would have our annual set-to over whether I would be allowed to do a narrative summary. This clashed with his banker's approach, but I knew the narrative was the only way that many board members would really grasp what the budget picture was all about.

The first item in the budgets I prepared for the American Heart Association and Mental Health Association was an estimated dollar value of the volunteer time contributed. It helped put the other budget items, particularly staff salaries, in perspective. My goal was to constantly increase the ratio of contributed time to staff salaries and other expenses. Although there are few comparisons available, I feel that a five-to-one ratio represents effective use of volunteers in relation to staff time. Obviously, this applies more to cause-oriented membership associations than to direct service organizations, but the exercise helps all nonprofit agencies to work hard at maximum volunteer utilization.

It's important to put a good deal of information into the budget, including the detailed breakdown of the various line items. For instance, within the line items of employee costs, it is important for the board members to know the relative costs of basic medical, major medical, retirement, social security, unemployment insurance, and any other benefits that are provided. Most board members won't want to get into that much detail, but at least it's there.

Budgeting dollars is only part of the necessary budgeting process. Budgeting staff time is perhaps even more important. Just as dollar resources have to be carefully directed toward the priorities determined by the board, so, too, must staff time. This sounds much more complicated that it really is. It's simply a matter of identifying the number of staff weeks that are available for actual work and matching these to the ongoing activities and special projects. If time sheets are coordinated with this, it's easy for a staff person to indicate the specific activities and projects to which time was devoted during the day. At the end of the month or quarter or year, it's possible to see if the staff time was actually spent in the patterns and on the priorities intended. This is also an important way to help board and committee members understand the current level of commitments. Otherwise, in the absence of this kind of specific information, boards and committees are almost too ready to add new projects or to assume that what they decided as priority is reflected by allocation of resources.

In addition to the board's own time, dollars and staff time are the two basic resources available to the board. They must be carefully measured and metered if they are to be directed in ways consistent with the agency's predetermined goals.

An organization should produce a monthly or at least quarterly income and expense statement, balance sheet, and budget status report. These should go to the board of directors in advance of their meetings. Copies should also be sent to the finance committee.

One of the problems for both boards and staff is the need for several different kinds of financial statements, for example: 1) those required in the standards; 2) those developed for management purposes; and 3) additional statements in a format required by governmental bodies, the United Way, foundations, or others.

I reconcile the requirements for different financial reports by starting with the system and information I need to manage the agency. I make sure that this is compatible with the standards and that my year-end reports can easily be recast into the format required by the standards and others. But the basic point is the need for a system that is conducive to sound day-to-day management.

In an understandable preoccupation with meeting the required accounting standards, too many agencies are trying to operate with the information that comes out of that system, and it just isn't adequate. For example, the standards will provide the organization and the public with information about the organization's proportional expenditures in certain fixed functional categories such as community services, public health education, and fundraising. But the manager and board will need to know more specifically how the money is being spent for nurses' seminars, traineeships, consecutive case conferences, and so forth. The "line" items (e.g. salaries, rent, and professional fees) required in the standards are necessarily broad so as to apply to many different organizations, and in that regard too, they have to be supplemented.

Operating and reserve funds that are available for short-term investments should be invested in savings accounts, certificates of deposit, treasury bills, or other reasonably liquid accounts. They should not be invested in common stocks. This includes all funds needed for operations or ready reserves. When common stocks are received as current contributions and are considered part of operating funds or ready reserves, they should be sold at time of receipt.

If the organization is fortunate to have endowment funds, these funds should be managed by a financial institution selected by the finance committee and approved by the board of directors. The investment policy should be established by the board. This can include a "combined income" or "total return" plan whereby the association, in consultation with the financial institution, establishes a fixed income that will be drawn from both income and principal. This allows for investment of some part of the fund in stocks as a hedge against inflation. The finance committee should do regular reviews of the fund, and members of the finance committee should be available to consider special advice from the financial institution.

Your most important financial report will be the annual audit, which should certainly go to the board with ample opportunity for discussion. At least some members of the board should fulfill the functions of an audit committee. Larger organizations will have a separate audit committee, but smaller groups may combine this with the work of the finance or executive committee or the full board.

The accounting firm of Price Waterhouse (now Pricewaterhouse Coopers) produced an excellent publication called "The Audit Committee: The Board of Trustees of Nonprofit Organizations and the Independent Accountant." Because the audit is so essential to knowing the financial state of your organization, I secured the firm's permission to present their description of the role of the audit committee:

1. Review of the financial statements with the independent accountants prior to recommending approval by the Board. The purpose of such a review is to determine that the independent accountants are satisfied with the disclosure and content of the financial statements and to obtain sufficient information from the auditors to facilitate analysis of the financial statements submitted to the entire board of trustees.

2. Appraisal of the effectiveness of the audit effort. This includes a discussion of the overall approach to and scope of the examination, with particular attention focused on those areas where either the committee or the independent accountants believe special emphasis is desirable or necessary. The responsibility for determination of the scope of auditing necessary for the formation of an opinion on the financial statements resides with the independent accountants, and that decision must be left to them. For this reason, the committee should not ask for nor be given detailed audit programs.

3. Determination through discussions with the independent accountants that no restrictions were placed by management on the scope of the examination or on its implementation. It is often appropriate for management representatives to allow the committee to meet alone at some point with the independent accountants. This is not intended in any sense to reflect adversely on the integrity of management; instead, it provides an additional margin of security in that there will be an opportunity for a complete interchange, without the inhibitions or restrictions that might exist if members of the management team were present. It also establishes for the record that the independent accountants were presented a chance to discuss with the committee any topics they might choose.

4. Inquiry into the effectiveness of the organization's management of financial and accounting functions, through discussions with the independent accountants and appropriate officers of the organization. Particular attention should be paid to the adequacy of internal controls over contributions and other sensitive areas.

5. Review of reports prepared by the independent accountants discussing weaknesses in internal control, organization structure and operations and containing recommendations to improve such weaknesses. There should be careful consideration of the action taken by management on the independent accountant's suggestions.

6. Recommendations of the appointment of independent accountants for the ensuing year. The actual appointment of the accounts should remain the responsibility of the full board. Management, through its day-to-day dealings with the independent accountants, normally is in the best position to evaluate the services provided, and its input to the committee should be given careful consideration when nominations for independent accountants are being considered. On the other hand, the committee should be certain that management's recommendations are objective and not designed to serve its own self-interest.

In my long experience with nonprofit organizations I've had some pretty rude awakenings and learned some pretty sad lessons. Let me summarize these lessons from the school of financial hard knocks. The lessons and the consequences apply to both board and staff.

- *Budget realistically.* It's too easy to get carried away with unduly optimistic income projections and unrealistic expectations. The resulting deficits and the horror of the budget cutbacks—particularly those that involve personnel—gradually teach the lesson that it's better to face reality and disappointment during the budgeting process than later.

- *Get regular monthly reports and study them carefully.* These reports should include at the very least the income and expense statement, balance sheet, and budget status report. A situation can change rapidly and unless caught early it is not reversible.

- *Be sure that the reports are accurate.* This may seem obvious, but I have lived with and through situations where, because of switchovers in accounting systems or turnovers of personnel in the accounting area, or just a poor accounting staff, reports have not been reliable. It's easy to assume that the staff director has a close enough view of the organization that the reports are not far out of kilter. Don't believe it! If there is any indication that the reports are not accurate, get that situation straightened out fast.

- *Insist on understanding the financial picture and the reports.* It's better to look silly than not to pursue a part of the financial picture or report that you don't quite understand. It's not sufficient that the executive committee understands it, or the treasurer or the accountant. The board members are ultimately responsible, and you have to understand it. Staff should be sure that reports are in a form that the trustees can understand and that the trustees feel free to ask questions.

- *Establish a close working relationship with the auditor.* For the staff, day-to-day access to the auditor is essential. Provide a realistic sum in the budget over and above the cost of the audit so that the staff director can feel free to consult regularly with the auditor on any financial management considerations. It's probably not practical for the board to work with the auditor, but the finance committee certainly should. If there is no finance committee, then the auditors should meet annually with the executive committee or board. It has always been my practice that at least part of that annual session of the finance committee and auditors is conducted in an executive session (without staff present). That bothers some executive directors and even some finance committee heads, but in a nonprofit organization it's too easy for the trustees to get far removed from understanding the financial side of the enterprise. It's important that at least those trustees who serve on the finance committee have an opportunity to learn firsthand that there are no barriers to getting the frank opinion of the auditors about the financial statements, internal controls, and the degree of cooperation given to the auditors.

- *Involve the auditor in establishing, or at least approving, your internal systems, including controls.* It's not enough to assume that the auditors are satisfied with your systems and controls simply because they provide you with a clean audit. They may be assuming too much, and, because it is essential that this area be properly organized, it is wise to involve them in setting up the system or at least regularly examining it in detail. Although these functions are usually delegated to staff, the board must be certain that they are fully and regularly carried out.

- *Make the most of the interest and knowledge of the treasurer and chairperson of the finance committee.* They can help tremendously in interpreting agency operations and finances to the board of directors. They will be useful in handling short-term investments or helping line up bank loans during low cash flow. But, most of all, you will need their hard-nosed, pragmatic, conservative fiscal judgment. They often provide unwelcome advice, but for that very reason it's important to have it immediately at hand.

- *Involve the key volunteer leaders in the development of the budget.* The budgeting function is often seen as an internal staff responsibility, but the person who will be serving as president when that budget is in effect can feel thwarted if he or she doesn't understand the budget and hasn't had an opportunity to see that it reflects priorities as the president and board perceive them.

- *Recognize how easily the budget can thwart or contradict the board's decisions on priorities.* The board can go through an elaborate process of determining new priorities, and yet, if the budget follows the same old pattern, the resources of dollars and staff are not likely to be converted to the new pattern of priorities.

- *Provide for some cushion in the budget.* I know from experience how important this is. It's so hard to cut a proposed budget to fit realistic projections of income that I can't routinely build in a 10- or even 5-percent cushion. On the other hand, I know that it is not possible to anticipate what emergencies will occur in the following fiscal year. A budget should have a contingency factor of 5 to 10 percent to be allocated, in small amounts, by the executive committee or board of directors for the unanticipated needs that arise during the year.

- *Provide for some basic reserves.* Nonprofit agencies should have reserves equal to at least one-half of one year's operating expenses, although usually not greater than one year's operating expenses.

This provides funds during low cash flow, a cushion against the almost inevitable occasional deficit, and some breathing room for emergencies. All this, of course, is in addition to fulfilling the basic purpose of a reserve—to help the agency survive a truly catastrophic period.

- ***Don't switch accounting systems until you are really on top of your information.*** There is always a temptation to help solve a current accounting problem by moving to a new system. My experience has been that you had better be very certain that you are getting accurate information from your current system before you start major adjustments. For example, I've seen a number of agencies run into terrible difficulty during a transition to computer operations. It's essential to be getting accurate information from your current system before and until the new system is functioning fully. It happens too often that board members who come from sophisticated operations will want to modernize the operations sooner than the staff is ready. They'll graciously offer to have their own organizations provide some of the equipment or computer time, and people who don't know very much about your operation will come in on a volunteer basis. I've even seen organizations switch over to an available software package, largely because it is available and seemed to work for someone else, without adequate consideration of whether it really fits. I had one board member send me to a week's training school that turned out to deal almost exclusively with large mainframe computers and other equipment utterly beyond our needs and finances.

- ***Realize that voluntary agencies are never going to get rich.*** Your people will sometimes wonder when that day will come when the agency won't be living hand-to-mouth or be facing an imminent financial crisis. I don't mean to unduly discourage you, but I don't think that the really effective voluntary agency dealing with a major public problem is ever going to be comfortable. The needs and pressures to do even more will always outweigh income. At least I know it's a way of life, and I'm not periodically disappointed that the tables haven't yet been turned.

- ***Remember that deficits are hell!***

This chapter has not attempted to describe the sophisticated procedures appropriate for many organizations. They can be found in such manuals as the AICPA's Guide, BoardSource's *Step-By-Step Nonprofit Financials*, and the Jossey-Bass/Wiley book *Financial and Accounting Guide for Not-for-Profit Organizations – Sixth Edition*, by Gross, Larkin, and McCarthy. Many voluntary organizations are as elaborate and sophisticated as the best businesses in their approach to financial planning, management of cash, decentralized budgeting, profit centers, and computerization of data so that they can provide trustees and staff with every possible analysis of financial operations and trends.

My purpose here is to try to provide you as a trustee with an understanding of the basic functions you must fulfill. However large or small the operation and however much sophisticated equipment is available to you, it still comes down to "What am I accountable for?" And at the top of the list is stewardship.

14

Ethics and Ethics Accountability

Since the first edition of this book was published, voluntary organizations, like most institutions, have begun to pay a great deal more attention to ethics and ethical behavior.

To ensure continued confidence and address issues raised by the well-publicized misbehavior of some voluntary and philanthropic institutions, the board of directors of INDEPENDENT SECTOR asked a broadly representative group of thirty persons to define as clearly as possible what this sector and all of its organizations should stand for. The committee included foundations, corporate giving programs, nonprofit leadership, legal scholars, journalists, consumer advocates, representatives of higher education and the religious community, government regulators of the sector, and ethicists. It was chaired by Ira Hirschfield, and I served as staff director, effectively assisted by Brian Foss.

With the permission of INDEPENDENT SECTOR, what follows are excerpts and summaries from the final statement: "Ethics and the Nation's Voluntary and Philanthropic Community: Obedience to the Unenforceable."

Defining, examining, and instilling ethical behavior is a vital role for board members. Whether your organization's interest is AIDS or ozone, the character of your organization ultimately must have an ethical component.

Obeying the law is the first and most obvious of our ethical obligations. It is "obedience to the unenforceable," however, as England's Lord Justice of Appeal John Fletcher Moulton said almost 100 years ago, that best measures the ethical behavior of individuals and their organizations. The true test of greatness, he explained, "is the extent to which the individuals composing the nation can be trusted to obey self-imposed law."

In the philanthropic/voluntary sector, public trust stems from our willingness to go beyond the law or even the spirit of the law. We act ethically because we have determined that it is the right thing to do.

The ethical behavior of an institution is the ultimate responsibility of its trustees. The responsibility is shared, however, with staff leaders and other staff and volunteers of the institution because it is critical that ethical considerations permeate every level of an organization.

Almost all voluntary organizations depend upon volunteers and donations, which is time and money people are not obligated to give. They do so voluntarily in the faith that trustees, staff, and other volunteer stewards will spend the money in the most judicious way to achieve the results for which the contribution was solicited. This is very much an act of faith.

Our groups do not face public elections and consequent reorganizations as government entities do. Nor do we have a bottom line of profit or loss determined by customers, as in the commercial sector. People put faith in us just because we are supposed to be charitable. The public assumes that we do our work with greater economy than government and with greater concern for individuals than either government or commerce. It believes we will work toward our goals in an honorable and humane way, with continuing regard for the rights and needs of individuals.

The public has faith in our stewardship, but it is also concerned about us. INDEPENDENT SECTOR's report "Keeping the Trust: Confidence in Charitable Organizations in an Age of Scrutiny" indicates that the public is trusting of voluntary organizations in the order of 65 percent. However, that study and others reveal that up to one-third of those surveyed either do not know how philanthropic and voluntary organizations spend their funds or do not know if they are spent wisely. Other studies confirm that the public is confused or growing wary about ethical standards in charitable organizations.

Clearly, abuses occur in the name of charity. The nonprofit sector has frauds and questionable operations. Unfortunately, their exposure gives the impression that the sector as a whole is losing its reliability. The public rightly demands the fullest examination of groups that ask for its support. When our institutions do not reflect high standards of openness, honesty, and public service, our contributors and clients feel ill-served; and because our organizations depend on public goodwill and participation, if public support is eroded, so is our capacity for public service.

The basic means by which you can ensure confidence in your organization is to demonstrate the quality of your leadership, which begins with full and consistent evidences that trustees, staff directors, and all other participants reflect habitually the ethics people have a right to expect of them, and that they make ethical practices part of the organization's culture.

Some trusteeship responsibilities relate to the organization's status as a formal legal entity, such as being sure that required reports are submitted to government. However, most expectations are of the higher order of Lord Moulton's "obedience to the unenforceable," such as making the contributor's dollar go as far as possible for the client and cause.

Ignorance of legal obligations leaves voluntary organizations vulnerable to oversights that often place them in jeopardy. Being charitable is no excuse for laxity. Voluntary and philanthropic organizations need to build specific internal processes that educate trustees about their legal obligations and provide timely procedures to meet them. For example, it is important to keep a checklist of all required reports, such as payments of social security allocations and payroll taxes withheld from compensation; the annual report to the federal government (Form 990) and similar state expectations; and to have the audit or other volunteer committee do an annual inventory to be sure all such requirements have been fulfilled. Their report should go to the board with ample time for the directors to be satisfied that *all* legal obligations have been met.

Most legal problems faced by trustees and other stewards are not the result of malfeasance. Good people believing in good things sometimes get into trouble. Yet, without checks, balances, and early warning signals, they rarely will escape spiraling legal difficulties.

It is important to acknowledge that at times, some voluntary organizations knowingly disobey certain laws, for example, by illegal sit-ins or by providing sanctuary for illegal aliens. An organization may feel such abridgements are necessary to fulfill its mission, but even courageous acts of conscience do not put people above the law. As indicated by Henry David Thoreau in "Civil Disobedience," one must believe so completely in such acts as to be willing to pay the consequences.

Much more challenging than following procedures set in law and regulation, however, is obeying the unenforceable. Many ethical situations are quite clear, but often there are no procedures to disclose them. For example, it is obvious that ethical considerations exist if an organization is doing business with a firm controlled by a staff member's spouse, but if no conflict of interest policy exists, and if there is no requirement for annual review of compliance with such a policy, how can the behavior be checked?

The first level of ethical behavior is to be concerned about obeying laws. The second is composed of those behaviors where one knows the right action but is tempted to take a different course. There is also a third level of consideration where decisions are not a contest between right and wrong but among competing options. These present us with touchy ethical dilemmas. Because we serve interests that often have scant resources, we inevitably must confront difficult choices and provide answers to ethical questions. For example, who will and will not receive scarce health services, such as dialysis?

An organization must have processes by which it can decide if the law is being obeyed, if thoughtful ethics are being practiced, and if tough ethical dilemmas are being openly considered and decided. Organizations that routinely utilize ethical decision-making practices will be much better prepared to handle a crisis if it hits.

INDEPENDENT SECTOR's report presents the following values and ethical behaviors as what this sector and its organizations have in common and should stand for.

- *Commitment* beyond self is at the core of a civil society.

- *Obedience to the laws*, including those governing tax-exempt philanthropic and voluntary organizations, is a fundamental responsibility of stewardship.

- *Commitment beyond the law*, to obedience to the unenforceable, is the higher obligation of leaders of philanthropic and voluntary organizations.

- *Commitment to the public good* requires those who presume to serve the public good to assume a public trust.

- *Respect for the worth and dignity of individuals* is a special leadership responsibility of philanthropic and voluntary organizations.

- *Tolerance, diversity, and social justice* reflect the independent sector's rich heritage and the essential protections afforded it.

- *Accountability to the public* is a fundamental responsibility of public benefit organizations.

- *Openness and honesty* in reporting, fundraising, and relationships with all constituencies are essential behaviors for organizations that seek and use public or private funds and that purport to serve public purposes.

- *Prudent application of resources* is a concomitant of public trust.

To provide more specific guidance, the report presents examples of illegal acts, unethical behaviors, and ethical dilemmas related to each of these values. It offers no answers to ethical dilemmas because organizations must struggle with such decisions on their own.

- *Commitment beyond self:*
  Example of an illegal act: The board agrees to sell property to a board member's spouse without competitive bidding and at a price below fair market value.

  Example of an unethical behavior: High, dishonest, or inappropriate expenses submitted for travel and meetings.

  Example of an ethical dilemma: A board member who heads the best public relations firm in town is the volunteer chair of your publicity committee and has a contract for some of the organization's advertising. Is this relationship acceptable, and if so, under what conditions?

- *Obedience of the laws, including those governing tax-exempt organizations:*
Example of an illegal act: A solicitation indicates that contributions are tax-deductible when they are not.

  Example of an unethical behavior: Board meetings often lack a quorum, but a few absentee board members are always willing to sign on to the decisions "to make it legal."

  Example of an ethical dilemma: The organization debates undertaking an illegal sit-in to call attention to the dangers of a new nuclear power plant. Legal counsel says that even if they succeed, there are likely to be arrests. What do you do?

- *Commitment to the public good:*
Example of an illegal act: A private foundation does not live up to the minimum payout requirement for grants.

  Example of an unethical behavior: Some long-term board members are listed as officers or committee chairpersons year after year, but they don't perform in those roles. They feel their years with the organization have earned them this visibility and control, and they are not about to step aside for some aggressive upstarts who want to upset the status quo.

  Example of an ethical dilemma: Should there be any compromise in your organization's standards or procedures if you receive a request for joint sponsorship of a project from another organization that recently responded favorably to your request for joint sponsorship?

- *Respect for the value and dignity of individuals:*
  Example of an illegal act: Hirings and promotions that deny equal employment opportunity in accord with the law.

  Example of an unethical behavior: A small executive committee of insiders makes all of the decisions for the board on the grounds that the issues are too sensitive or complex to bring to the full board.

  Example of an ethical dilemma: What do you do when an ad hoc group of the organization's clients demands to meet with your board to present grievances, and the staff says that if the board caves in to these chronic complainers it will quit?

- *Tolerance, diversity, and social justice:*
  Example of an illegal act: A staff person is identified as a leader of a conservative fundamentalist sect and is dismissed from his research position.

  Example of an unethical behavior: No minority persons are on a social service board serving minority neighborhoods.

  Example of an ethical dilemma: Should a corporate foundation give grants to a company's potential detractors or to causes not well thought of by some employees?

- *Openness and honesty:*
  Example of an illegal act: Required government reports are not filed or are filed with inaccurate information.

  Example of an unethical behavior: The combination of four grants given to the organization by different donors covers 150 percent of your education director's time, salary, and space.

  Example of an ethical dilemma: Does the grantmaker tell an applicant the application was terrible, and does the applicant tell the grantmaker the process was rude?

- *Accountability to the public:*
Example of an illegal act: Form 990 is not available to the public.

Example of an unethical behavior: For the fifth year in a row, the fundraising appeal talks only about plans and not about what's been done to date.

Example of an ethical dilemma: Should a nonprofit that espouses full disclosure but is dealing with a very controversial cause publish its list of contributors?

- *Efficiency and effectiveness:*
Example of an illegal act: To deal with a worsening cash shortage, money withheld from employees' payments for federal income tax is not turned over to the IRS.

Example of an unethical behavior: Services are targeted to clients with the fewest needs because the organization wants to show funders high numbers of people served successfully.

Example of an ethical dilemma: Board meetings are crisp and brief but do cover all required actions. Board members generally don't feel involved and certainly don't feel inspired. The chairperson takes pride in how businesslike the governance is but ignores declines in enthusiasm, attendance, and reenlistment.

- *Prudent application of resources:*
Example of an illegal act: The organization's copying and fax machines are used routinely by a friendly candidate for public office.

Example of an unethical behavior: In lieu of salary, the staff director prefers a percentage of all funds raised.

Example of an ethical dilemma: The all-volunteer organization recognizes that to hire its first executive director will absorb all the money on hand and in sight. Half the board argues that all the time and money will go to support the position with nothing left for programs, and the other half says it's a necessary investment in future growth. What should you do?

Every organization should adopt at least a simple organizational credo. The extent of each statement will depend upon the size and capacity of the organization, but it need not be elaborate. An example follows:

ORGANIZATIONAL CREDO

We believe that as stewards of (organization), which has been established for public benefit and has legal standing for that purpose, we have accepted a public trust to abide by high standards of performance and ethical behavior.

Adoption of a credo will be effective only if it initiates a conversation within and throughout your organization. Trustees and staff leaders must involve all those associated with the organization to participate in setting an ethical environment.

Your organization should take enough time, at least once a year, for an *internal* ethics audit or self-evaluation. The examination should ask at least three questions:

1. Have the requirements for our legal standing been fulfilled, such as submitting all required reports and with full and honest disclosure?

2. What, if any, activities or practices of the board, staff, or organization are there that might be contrary to our organization's credo and articulated core values?

3. Are there changes in the social, demographic, or economic contexts of our interest that compel us to make different and/or more difficult ethical choices? If so, what changes are there that deserve notice?

Further, your organization should undertake an *external* ethics audit or evaluation every few years, using trained staff or personnel from other voluntary and philanthropic organizations, universities, or consultant organizations. An outside look can prevent ethical processes from becoming so routine as to be irrelevant, introduce different perspectives and analyses, and affirm good practice.

Beyond a credo and regular examinations of practice, larger organizations, at least, should develop more complete codes of ethics and/or standards or policies that govern the organization's ethical performance. These should include a timetable and process for the evaluation of performance in accord with the codes or policies.

In developing and implementing ethical standards, your organization should involve all of your constituencies, internally and externally. Each needs an opportunity to shape the organization's values and ethics and the modes of compliance to them. Maximum meaningful involvement is the single most important step to ensure that your organization is true to its values and the public trust. Trustees open the door. The opportunity to participate depends upon your receptivity to making this process an open, honest, and essential mission.

Your organization should also do everything possible to be certain the documents and the values they reflect become part of the culture of the total organization. For example, orientation sessions for new board members, staff, and volunteers should include review of the credo and other documents related to values, standards, and ethical practices.

It is essential that trustees be involved in the process and ultimately responsible for approval of such reports. Many other groups and publishers have begun to call attention to the ethical expectations described in INDEPENDENT SECTOR's report. For example: "Developing an Ethics Program: A Case Study for Nonprofit Organizations," by Charles E. M. Kolb, for BoardSource; "Leading With Values: Achieving Ethical Fitness," a CD-ROM-based Ethics Training for Nonprofits, produced by the Institute for Global Ethics in cooperation with the Alliance for Nonprofit Management, INDEPENDENT SECTOR, BoardSource, and National Council of Nonprofit Associations.

All of the steps to develop, indicate, and evaluate ethical practices should be seen as affirming the good an organization does and helping those involved with it to be proud of what they do. This is an opportunity to express respect for individuals and causes, to encourage creativity, and to create a committed community.

After the above chapter had been completed, we learned that INDEPENDENT SECTOR was preparing a revised edition of its ethics report for release in 2003. Therefore, for the latest information, please order "Obedience to the Unenforceable: Ethics and the Nation's Voluntary and Philanthropic Community, Revised 2003, INDEPENDENT SECTOR, 1200 Eighteenth Street, NW, Suite 200, Washington, DC 20036 or www.independentsector.org.

15

Evaluating Results

Voluntary agencies are usually so busy doing that there isn't time (or it seems a poor use of time) to become involved with serious evaluation. At some point though, someone inside or outside the organization is going to want to know if the effort is reasonably successful. Then you'll be pressed to provide some justification and assurance. It is to be hoped that you, as a trustee, will be the first to ask.

A medical researcher friend of mine, long active in voluntary agencies, has this wonderful description of how nonprofit groups generally evaluate their results: "Any group as bright as we are which has worked as long and hard as we have must have done a lot of good." Don't dismiss too hastily this pleasantly cynical characterization of our approach to evaluation. When those doubting Thomases begin to raise questions about your beloved organization, you may well find yourself reacting instinctively, and maybe even a bit testily, with a rather subjective, "It must be the most obvious thing in the world that any group as bright as we are. . . ."

In "Better Performance From Nonprofits," Cecily Cannon Selby, former national director of the Girl Scouts, made somewhat the same point: "Another assumption, not invalid on its face but leading to many pitfalls, is that volunteering is a good in itself. Because I am a volunteer and doing something gratis for others, I am doing something good in itself, and anything I do in this role must be good."

There is the likelihood, however, that at some point this may not be good enough for some other members of the board or for some contributors, or maybe even for you. You will then want to have a more objective measurement of whether it's all worthwhile or whether at least you're getting all the results you should.

Evaluation doesn't have to be complicated. It can be as basic as deciding what you want to achieve by the end of the year and then figuring out later if you got there. At its simplest, evaluation starts with an attainable goal to be accomplished at a realistic date, with a prior commitment to stop what you're doing on that date to look back to see if your goal was actually reached. The sad reason so many organizations don't follow this simple procedure is that they don't even start with a plan; therefore, they don't have a specific goal or deadline to check back on. My formula is that fuzzy goals equal fuzzy evaluation, and unfortunately, the combination usually adds up to fuzzy performance.

In Chapter 9, I said that much of the planning in our agencies is characterized by the following attitude: "We're going to do as much good as we possibly can, and we can't be expected to do any more."

I also said that specialists in planning have a way of making the process so involved that we tend to dismiss their recommendations as being beyond the resources and sophistication of our voluntary operations. The same thing happens with evaluation.

If what you see when you look back isn't pleasing, you'll automatically begin asking why, and this will be the beginning of a more effective marshaling of resources to accomplish the things that really are most important.

At this point, any evaluators or planners reading this are probably tearing their hair out because their science has been stripped to such nakedness. Nevertheless, planning and evaluation can be easy, and they can be simple. Earlier I quoted the Peter Principle, "If you don't know where you're going, you'll end up someplace else." An evaluation sequel might be: "If you don't know where you've been, how do you know you got there?"

There should be a built-in mechanism for self-evaluation. As stated previously, this can be as simple as at the end of the year taking a look to see if your goals have in fact been achieved. This is the most basic form of self-evaluation and should be a routine part of every organization's operations.

In addition, there should be some mechanism by which the board can periodically take a fuller look at the organization's operations and activities. For instance, this review should determine whether or not basic planning and evaluation are being done annually. You'll find that these, too, can be as simple or as complex as the operation itself.

Peter Szanton has produced a helpful guide for BoardSource called "Evaluation and the Nonprofit Board" that includes "some key questions to ask during the evaluation process," such as:

- *What is our purpose?* To evaluate is to measure how well an organization is achieving its purpose. So this first question is fundamental: What is our purpose? What are we seeking to achieve? If the organization has a mission statement and is content with it, that statement will provide at least a general answer to the question of purpose.

- *How well are we achieving our purpose?* Almost certainly, some goals are being met, some homeless *are* being housed, some minority students *are* receiving an advanced education, some illnesses *are* being treated, the opera *was* able to mount a new production. But how fully and efficiently are those ends being attained?

- *Is there a better way?* Is the organization achieving its mission as fully as its resources permit, or might there be better ways of gaining its ends?

Periodically—at least every five years—you should arrange for an outside evaluation. This is most easily arranged if you are part of a national organization. For various reasons, you may resist having representatives of a national board or staff do the evaluation. If that's the case, you can put together a team from your sister associations, which really constitutes a peer review. If that avenue isn't available, it shouldn't be difficult to put together a willing and able team from your own community. In every town there are scores if not hundreds of people who have had unusual success in nonprofit activities. Ask two or three of the best staff directors and most experienced board volunteers from other groups to perform this function for you. They will be proud to be asked.

An effective evaluation will depend on the degree to which measurable standards are at hand, which begins with knowing what constitutes acceptable performance and better.

In an invaluable article, "How Can Businessmen Evaluate the Management of Voluntary Welfare Agencies?," Earle Lippincott and Elling Aannestad state, ". . . if the basic organizational components of the agency are operating effectively you can assume that the output is likely to be worthwhile." They acknowledged that this isn't an exact equation, but they believe, for example, ". . . if the Board and the basic committees are functioning—including regular meetings with quorums present—it is likely the agency is not wasting its time."

In looking for operating standards, Lippincott and Aannestad asked the following questions:

1. Are the Board and staff set up to work effectively?

2. How well defined are the needs served by the agency and its program for meeting these needs?

3. Are adequate financial safeguards and sound controls maintained for fundraising?

4. Is the agency's work related to that of the national organization and of other planning groups in the field?

5. Is the agency doing a good job of what it is set up to do?

6. How many other agencies are trying to do all or parts of the same job?

7. Does the agency function in proper relationship to government agencies?

When I was the director of the American Heart Association in California, we agreed with Lippincott and Aannestad that one can be encouraged if the basic operation seems to be functioning. We recognized, however, that this doesn't assure that the end product is really good or is even as good as it should be. Therefore, we added two elements. First, we identified the basic activities that we believed a chapter of the American Heart Association should be handling well. Second, we acknowledged that one of the great things about voluntary agencies is their role as innovators. Obviously certain activities can't be anticipated, so we gave a whopping one-third of the total score to those unusual things that the chapter might be doing over and above the basics.

As a result, our standards were divided into three parts: 1) "Basic Organization" (such as board makeup, meetings, and turnover), 2) "Basic Activities" (such as an information and referral program, and at least one seminar for general practitioners each year), and 3) "Additional Activities." A chapter was evaluated every three years by a peer group of board members from other chapters. This had many intended and desirable results, but it also had a side benefit: The board members doing the evaluation learned a good deal about how to improve their own chapters.

Most of your basic standards are probably already at hand or are suggested by the performance standards published by the BBB (Better Business Bureau) in "Wise Giving Alliance Standards for Charitable Accountability." I included some of them in the beginning of Part II, in discussing the role of the board and board members because, as I said, "It is helpful to start with the standards of performance by which organizations are held accountable and then work backward to how the board can be sure that the organization passes those tests." I feel strongly about this point and hope you will consider it central to the subject of evaluation as well. Please also see Appendix B for a fuller look at the Standards.

One of the frustrations for business people serving on voluntary organization boards is that it is so hard to define and measure success. Nonprofits will never have the simple measure of corporate bottom-line profits. A serious consequence is that too many nonprofit organizations assume, therefore, that other business standards and practices don't apply either. In her article, "Better Performance from Nonprofits," Selby says that "the same businessman who would not conceive of going into the toothpaste business without identifying the merits of his products, identifying the market to which the product must be sold, and developing a plan to bring the product to market, will work in a voluntary organization without taking the same steps with respect to its 'product.'"

In *Management Control in Nonprofit Organizations*, Robert M. Anthony and Regina Herzlinger of the Graduate School of Business Administration at Harvard put it this way:

> All organizations use inputs to produce outputs. An organization's effectiveness is measured by the extent to which outputs accomplish its objectives, and its efficiency is measured by the relationship between inputs and outputs.

In a profit-oriented organization the amount of profit provides an overall measure of both effectiveness and efficiency. In many non-profit organizations, however, outputs cannot be measured to quantitative terms.... The absence of a satisfactory, single, overall measure of performance that is comparable to the profit measure is the most serious management control problem in a nonprofit organization. (It is incorrect to say that the absence of the profit motive is the central problem; rather, it is the absence of the profit *measure*. . . .)

One of the large problems facing boards attempting to evaluate performance is the confusion about how much voluntary organizations should be like businesses. Businessmen and women who have not served extensively with voluntary organizations will so desperately want the organization to mirror what they know best and to come closer to a "bottom line" that they will be extremely impatient with their nonprofit organizations. This has led them, in fairly significant numbers, to assume and claim that voluntary organizations generally are managed poorly. It has become routine to hear such observations as, "These do-gooders and bleeding hearts just don't know how to manage," or "If we could just get more management discipline into these cause-oriented organizations, they would be far more effective."

It's my own observation that these perceptions are inaccurate and unfair. Voluntary organizations are like businesses and other human institutions in that about one-third are models of excellence—beautiful examples of caring and daring and innovation and efficiency. For what they are supposed to be in our pluralistic society, they are our models of excellence. One-third are average—good to fair—and one-third are poorly managed and generally ineffective.

Senator Robert Packwood, who chaired the Senate Commerce Committee and therefore had a good opportunity to observe all three sectors, said that on the basis of his regular dealings with government, business, and the nonprofit world, he found that foundations and voluntary organizations are by far the most reliable—that is, the most certain to do what they were established to do and what society expects of them.

Management consultant Peter Drucker was once asked by a business reporter, "What's the most effective organization with which you've ever worked?" Obviously, the inquirer assumed that the answer would be a business corporation such as General Electric, Xerox, or Hewlett-Packard. Drucker thought a moment and replied, "The Girl Scouts." The reporter laughed and said that he hoped Drucker would be willing to give a serious answer, and Drucker responded that he was absolutely serious in believing that the Girl Scouts was the most effective group with which he had worked. He pointed out that if you took that many dedicated volunteers, with a professional staff oriented and trained to increase the usefulness of the volunteers, and you pointed all of that energy and commitment toward an important social purpose, such as the development of women and girls, those were clearly the ingredients for effectiveness and excellence.

That episode points up a large part of the misunderstanding about excellence in voluntary organizations. Before we can judge performance, we have to have a clearer grasp of what we're looking for. In the case of nonprofit organizations, we need to have a much better grasp of the uniqueness of these organizations, both in the social role they fulfill and in the ways they do it. If we simply apply efficiency as our standard, we fail to distinguish special characteristics of dynamic voluntary organizations. Nonprofit organizations can learn a great deal from businesses about good management, bottom-line discipline, people development, evaluation of results, and much more, but these are often not their primary ingredients for excellence.

In a *Wall Street Journal* article, "Managing the Third Sector," Drucker wrote:

> Both the businessman and the civil servant tend to underrate the difficulty of managing service institutions. The businessman thinks it's all a matter of being efficient, the civil servant thinks it's all a matter of having the right procedures and controls. Both are wrong—service institutions are more complex than either businesses or government agencies. . . .

There's another factor of uniqueness that comes a little closer to the business model, which involves results measured against costs. In Drucker's *Harvard Business Review* piece, "What Business Can Learn From Nonprofits," he underscores how much the voluntary groups accomplish with the combination of maximum caring and minimum cost. He admires their effective utilization of volunteers and boards and their ability to stretch a dollar so much farther than businesses. He says, for example, "As a rule, nonprofits are more money-conscious than business enterprises are. They talk and worry about money much of the time because it is so hard to raise and because they always have so much less of it than they need."

I once compared businesses and voluntary organizations with Andrew Heiskell, former chief executive officer of Time Inc., who has probably had as much exposure to both sides as anyone, and he said that he has come to believe that "voluntary organizations demand much more of themselves than most businesses, and they get much more out of their boards, staff and dollars."

Keeping volunteers involved and growing in enthusiasm and effectiveness is different than business. They are unpaid, even more independent than employees, and hopefully there are far more of them per staff supervisor. Other factors that make voluntary groups quite different include the need to constantly achieve maximum community involvement, fundraising, board participation as both policymakers and as part of the team of doers, no advertising budget, and far lower salaries.

In the March/April 1989 issue of *Across the Board* (published by the Conference Board) several former business executives indicated that they thought their transfer to full-time roles on the voluntary side would be "a piece of cake," but all of them had retreated to the corporate ranks as a result of the dizzying complexity of working with artists, faculty, independent-minded boards, fundraising expectations, and staff and resources totally inadequate to the obligations.

I've worked with some chaotic, break-all-the-rules community organizations that business observers thought were the epitome of poor management, but which were perfect examples of dynamic associations mobilizing people to deal with a very real need or aspiration. Management people will tend to focus on the fact that the organization doesn't have bylaws, hasn't been keeping minutes, or is living hand to mouth, but a community organizer will see citizens mobilizing other citizens to really make a difference. A great many voluntary organizations are both dynamic and efficient, but if I had to settle on one characteristic, it would be the former.

Even in larger organizations, there's a tendency to overlook the unique functions of citizen service, advocacy, and education. When I was National Director of the Mental Health Association, new board members from the corporate side would invariably react that the board was too large, that there were too few internal administrative staff members, or that, for efficiency, we should consider merging with the retardation association. They didn't understand the need to achieve maximum feasible involvement and the need to keep citizens mobilized around causes they care passionately about.

There's another area of strain between voluntary organizations and their business trustees, and often with their funders as well, that would be humorous were it not so serious. Rarely are voluntary organizations allowed to build a realistic reserve, and even one year of deficit budgeting is viewed as a clear indication of poor management. Even the best businesses have deficit years, but woe to the voluntary agency manager who, though dealing with urgent causes, has a year or two of red ink.

There was great interest in the book *In Search of Excellence: Lessons From America's Best Run Companies*, by Thomas Peters and Robert Waterman, in which they described some of the sensitive and sensible ingredients of good management. At the heart of their book is the chapter entitled "Back to Basics," which includes these subheadings:

- Managing Ambiguity and Paradox

- A Bias for Action

- Close to the Customer

- Autonomy and Entrepreneurship

- Productivity Through People

- Hands-On, Value-Driven

- Stick to the Knitting

- Simple Form, Lean Staff

- Simultaneous Loose-Tight Properties

These subheadings describe the attributes that have characterized the best of voluntary organizations for hundreds of years. Their primary chapter is even entitled "Man Waiting for Motivation!"

Cecily Selby has examined the similarities and differences between profit and nonprofit organizations. Her findings help to remove the excuses proffered by nonprofit organizations when they should be performing in a "businesslike" way, but she also helps us to understand the areas where comparisons are not practical or fair. She says:

The altruistic, cause-related motivation that gives nonprofit organizations their great strength can be their downfall if it is not understood and appropriately handled. If these organizations are treated as illegitimate rather than legitimate, their innate operational differences from those in business will emerge as functional weaknesses. The uniqueness of this sector must be built on, and management techniques and related training programs that are adapted to nonprofits' special characteristics must be better developed.

The three "key differences" that Selby finds between nonprofit and profit organizations are: 1) "the bottom line"; 2) "the confusion in direct-line accountability" (for example, she asks, ". . . in a board appointed program committee on which volunteers serve, is it the committee or the staff that is accountable for the function, and can staff be accountable for what volunteers fail to do?"); and 3) "the mixed allegiance of many professionals in voluntary organizations who do not see themselves as part of the organizational hierarchy, at least in terms of accountability." She cites as examples the university professor and other intellectuals and artists who have their "own sense of creative integrity—an accountability that can override all others."

She concludes by calling for nonprofit organizations to be more effective, but not always with the business model in mind:

> In using the term nonprofit, which refers to a financial balance sheet only, perhaps we obscure the essence of this sector of our society, which is indeed to be profitable to citizens, business and government—to benefit its constituents, its clients and its employees. This sector has found, and one hopes we'll continue to find, new and better ways to preserve and enhance pluralism, voluntarism, and the distinctiveness of art, intellect and charity.

While I agree entirely with Selby, I also know that your likely frustration and mine is that we are not well along in defining those differences and determining how to measure excellence in such intangibles as the promotion of pluralism or art. In "Evaluating Nonprofit Activity" (from *The Nonprofit Organization Handbook*, edited by Tracy D. Connors), David Horton Smith says that people hide behind the statement, "You can't quantify virtue and helpfulness," but he asks how we really know if "the virtue really helps anybody?"

If evaluating nonprofit activity in general is difficult, it gets downright tormenting when you try to determine the results in programs related to advocacy, citizen education, good government, or other intangibles. With tongue in cheek, Anthony and Herzinger suggest that the way to measure the output of religious organizations might be "souls saved per pew-hour preached." The late Paul Ylvisaker, former dean of Harvard's Graduate School of Higher Education, took that a step further and said, "It's hard to evaluate the success of a church when you're denied access to the final judgment!"

The usual response to this difficulty is either to do nothing or to change the program focus toward more measurable activities just because they are measurable. In the first draft of the United Way of America's Services Identification System (UWASIS), there was a commendable attempt to quantify all program activities, but the colossal early mistake, later corrected, was to give the most measurable functions the highest priority. Advocacy and public education efforts were assigned the lowest ranking. When those of us in the mental health field challenged this overly simple determination, United Way acknowledged that advocacy was our most important service; but by then many local United Ways were penalizing us because they too had gone overboard on the "body count" emphasis.

Even when an organization can point to major advances in the directions of its advocacy and education programs, it's hard to prove cause and effect. Some organizations grossly exaggerate their impact on, say, a school board or Congress. Where is the middle ground?

At INDEPENDENT SECTOR (IS) we were particularly eager to get a handle on an organization's effectiveness in hard-to-measure categories—for example, the results of advocacy initiatives designed to influence government practices or our ability to help develop greater research activity in and on the sector. We thought we should start with some of our own activities and try to study the results in ways that might be replicable by our members and others.

In the course of our search, we came across a distinguished sociologist, Linda Fisher of Chicago, some of whose experience was relevant to our concerns and who was interested in working with us to develop and test a likely model. It doesn't do her or the committee justice to be so brief, but in essence, she concluded that though we might not achieve absolutely definitive answers, we could get pretty close to them via a four-pronged approach. She developed and tested a set of objective questions, then sought out and interviewed four categories of informed people. For example, when the objective was to learn if

IS had *really* had a significant influence in the passing or blocking of legislation, she would interview: 1) key legislators and staff from the committees in which the legislation was considered; 2) reporters who had considerable experience in covering that beat and were doing so when the specific legislation was under consideration; 3) people likely to have an informed opinion who were recommended by the first two groups; and 4) IS members who depended on us to be effective in the issues under review.

Linda pointed out that if we wanted to appear more scientific, we could put a numerical ranking on answers to multiple-choice questions and provide a score. But we decided, with her agreement, simply to ask knowledgeable people whether they felt that INDEPENDENT SECTOR had been "singularly influential, very effective, effective, somewhat effective, or useless." The interviews were also designed to elicit what it was that seemed to make us effective or ineffective and what we could have done to be more effective.

The process helped sharpen our planning so that we could be even more specific about what we were trying to achieve and evaluate.

For five years, INDEPENDENT SECTOR engaged in another large project designed to determine much more accurately the characteristics of organizations that clients, funders, boards, peers, and others all considered models of excellence. The results of that project are now in book form, *Profiles of Excellence: Studies of Effectiveness of Nonprofit Organizations*, authored by the project directors, E.B. Knauft, Renee Berger, and Sandra T. Gray, and published by Jossey-Bass. The authors summarized their findings:

> Picture a professional orchestra. Its musicians read notes proficiently, play their instruments well and practice long hours together. But it takes much more to turn a credible group of music makers into a world-class symphony orchestra.
>
> The same is true for a nonprofit organization. It takes more than a good board, a competent director and solid financial controls to differentiate the truly great organization from the larger universe of merely good ones. Our hallmarks of excellence are no substitute for sound management practices. Rather, they are the "something extra" that makes all the difference. . . .

Four overreaching characteristics appear repeatedly in the best nonprofit organizations. These hallmarks [of excellence] reflect more than sound management practices, good staff and effective programs—although all are important components of excellence. But the very best groups consistently manifest something more—a clear and tangible "value added."

The hallmarks of excellence in nonprofit organizations are:

1. A clearly articulated sense of mission that serves as the focal point of commitment for board and staff and is the guidepost by which the organization judges its success and makes adjustments in course over time;

2. An individual who truly leads the organization and creates a culture that enables and motivates the organization to fulfill its mission;

3. An involved and committed volunteer board that relates dynamically with the chief staff officer and provides a bridge to the larger community; and

4. An ongoing capacity to attract sufficient financial and human resources.

The book examines in detail each of these "hallmarks" and provides case studies of organizations that became excellent because of them.

If you don't know how to evaluate a rather involved activity, turn to your college sociology department or other social scientists who are likely to be quite skilled and helpful in identifying ways you can get more objective readings of your results.

You can also turn to various publications for advice on objective evaluation. For example, David Horton Smith in "Evaluating Nonprofit Activity" (in *The Nonprofit Organization Handbook*, edited by Tracy D. Connors) shares these helpful observations:

Social science research makes it quite clear that although we may all be pretty good at evaluating other people and programs with which we are familiar, we tend to overestimate the worth of ourselves and our own programs, organizations, contributions, and so on. I may be able to evaluate your contribution fairly accurately and you may be able to do likewise for me, but we would probably fail to be objective about ourselves. That is why physicians do not try to treat themselves.

Hence, the next step up the quality continuum is to have the evaluation of an informed, unbiased outside observer. Just by having an outsider—one not directly involved with the program or organization being evaluated—one has guaranteed a certain amount of objectivity, other things being equal. The problem, of course, is to make sure that the outsider gets enough or has enough information about your NPO program in order to make an informed evaluation. Yet even if this matter of informing the outside evaluator/rater is dealt with successfully, there are still likely to be various idiosyncratic biases that characterize the single outside evaluator. Still, the process of engaging and working with a single outside evaluator can have a great positive impact on an organization, especially if his/her visits bring together people and groups who do not normally meet or who do not discuss evaluation seriously if they do. Similarly, the single outside evaluator can lead the program/organization to begin to gather new and better data on themselves, consider alternative programs, spell out goals and priorities more clearly, and so on.

Fortunately, social science research has been able to show a simple solution to this problem. It turns out that if you take the evaluation of several informed outside observers, their individual biases tend to cancel each other out to a substantial degree so that their collective evaluation (submitted individually and independently—by secret ballot, so to speak) is very reliable on the whole. Experiments have shown that the largest gains in objectivity and reliability of evaluation are made as one goes from one informed outside observer to, say, five. After that additional members of the panel are still important up to about ten or twelve raters. Beyond this point, there is relatively little to be gained by simply adding more raters to the panel or team.

Evaluation can be sophisticated and technical, and both planning and evaluation are vital management skills that, in complex operations, will need to be carried to a very technical level. The only reason they were stripped of some of their status earlier in this chapter was to make the point that most things boil down to common sense, and if people can start there, they actually will get started.

For larger and more complex organizations, the planning and evaluation process will require the skills of a specialist to take advantage of the refined methods that have been developed for more scientific examination and determination of goals, the quantification of these goals, and an exact evaluation that automatically identifies the impediments standing in the way of maximum fulfillment of goals.

Another example of advanced evaluation involves the accreditation standards and evaluations of such groups as the American Association of Museums and the accrediting bodies related to secondary schools and to colleges and universities. In the case of museums, over the years peer groups have agreed on "basic standards" and "standards of excellence," and each museum is visited by an accrediting team at least every ten years to see if it meets or continues to meet the standards.

The sophisticated arrangements I have been talking about are obviously beyond the needs and resources of most voluntary organizations. It is important to make clear that, however simple or complicated the nonprofit endeavor, there have been developed and continue to be developed competent ways to measure results.

The best checklist I've found for evaluating the board's own performance was developed by Father Thomas J. Savage and The Cheswick Center. The checklist, originally published in "The Cheswick Process: Seven Steps to a More Effective Board," is reproduced at the end of this chapter.

The inclusion of Cheswick's board checklist underscores how important I believe it is for boards to evaluate their own performance. It's the most important phase in the whole review process. As you move out to the broader organization, I hope I've provided some guidelines and examples for that fuller review.

One quick way to take a look at your organization might be to match yours against a profile of effective voluntary organizations that I developed after years of trying to figure out why some voluntary organizations failed and others succeeded. The successful ones have these characteristics:

- A cause worth getting excited about.

- An ability to generate funds to do the job.

- Programs that can in fact do something for the cause.

- Adequate attention to morale in order to keep the undertaking spirited and vigorous even when the immediate tasks are not.

- Appropriate emphasis on increasing the number of citizens involved.

- Ability to keep the volunteers in charge even after the operation is staffed.

- Flexibility to respond effectively to new problems and opportunities and to fit the profile of "ad-hocracy," which must increasingly characterize the useful ongoing organization.

- A capacity to keep the real mission in focus no matter how frenzied things become or how great the pressure to move into new areas. This means that all important decisions are made with the organization's "reason for being" kept clearly in the forefront.

- Vision to see beyond the horizon, along with a sensitivity to human needs and an almost contradictory toughness to build an organization capable of translating the vision and sensitivity into change.

Despite the fact that planning and evaluation can become exceedingly complicated and sophisticated, they start with the basics of articulating goals, establishing timetables, and looking back at a later date to evaluate the progress or lack of it.

In the future, you will be able to say, "Any group as bright and dedicated as we are, which has worked as long and hard as we have, *and which has been so conscientious in evaluating our results*, has obviously done a great deal of good."

Congratulations. You're special.

Sample Questionnaires for Board Self-Evaluation

Board Self-Rating Schedule, Long Form	Excellent	Good	Fair	Poor	Non-existent	No Opinion
Legal Framework						
1. Statements in the governing documents (charter, deed of trust, bylaws, etc.) setting forth the function and duties of the Board are:						
2. Statements in the governing documents outlining the role and responsibilities of individual members of the Board are:						
3. Statements in the governing documents outlining the role and responsibilities of the chair of the Board are:						
4. Conformance of public warranties of the institution, express or implied, as evidenced by catalogs, guarantees, advertisements, solicitations, etc., to statements in the governing document is:						
Structure of the Board						
1. The size of the Board in relation to the needs of the institution is:						
2. The composition of the Board with regard to background and demographic factors, personal and professional interest, talents and points of view is:						
3. The usual method of selection of new board members is:						
4. The orientation process for new board members is:						
5. Retirement provisions for board members are:						
6. The committee structure of the Board is:						
Comprehension of the Board						
1. Understanding by board members of the purposes and objectives of the institution is:						
2. Comprehension by board members of the Board's role is:						
3. Comprehension by board members of their responsibilities is:						
4. Understanding by board members of their responsibilities is:						
5. The Board's recognition that mere compliance with the law does not assure good management is:						

*Reproduced from "Seven Steps to a More Effective Board," by Thomas J. Savage, S.J., with permission © 1982, revised May 1994, The Cheswick Center, Boston, MA, National Press Publications

Sample Questionnaires Continued

Board Self-Rating Schedule	Excellent	Good	Fair	Poor	Non-existent	No Opinion
6. The Board's knowledge of and familiarity with the institutional structure of the institution is:						
7. The Board's perception and understanding of key factors in the success of the institution is:						
8. The Board's comprehension of the interests of the several constituencies with which the institution deals is:						
9. The supply of information regarding external developments—legal, economic, sociological, statutory, etc.—that may affect board decisions, and which is given to board members is:						
10. Board member's degree of interest in and knowledge of:						
Continuous learning is:						
Broad economic development is:						
Politics and public policy issues is:						
International affairs is:						
Accounting is:						
Finance is:						
Marketing is:						
Management and leadership issues is:						
Technology is:						
Other (as appropriate to the institution)						
11. The Board's comprehension of the present position of the institution						
In its "industry" is:						
In its community is:						
12. Ability of the Board to plan for the role of the institution five years in the future in view of current social, economic, and political developments is:						
13. Familiarity of board members with provisions in the bylaws protecting or indemnifying them in the event suits are brought against them personally is:						

Sample Questionnaires Continued

Board Self-Rating Schedule	Excellent	Good	Fair	Poor	Non-existent	No Opinion
Practices of the Board						
1. The Board's manual of Policies and Procedures is:						
2. The frequency of Board meetings in relation to organizational needs is:						
3. Attendance of board members at meetings is:						
4. The pre-meeting package of informational material forwarded to the Board in preparation for meetings is:						
5. Financial and other reports presented to the Board, appraised in terms of:						
Intelligibility, are:						
Completeness, are:						
Conformity to the needs of the Board, are:						
6. Record-keeping of board meetings is:						
7. Conformity of board records with legal requirements is:						
8. The method by which the Board receives the report of the outside auditors, including the opportunity to discuss the report with the auditors, is:						
9. The Board's practices as regards:						
Changes to amendments of bylaws are:						
Election of executive officers of the institution are:						
Grants of powers of attorney are:						
Changes in financial reserves or endowments are:						
Establishing or altering pension plans are:						
10. Methods by which the Board periodically establishes short or long run goals for the institution are:						
11. The use of key executives in making presentations to the Board is:						

Sample Questionnaires Continued

Board Self-Rating Schedule	Excellent	Good	Fair	Poor	Non-existent	No Opinion
12. The use of inspection trips by the Board into different departments, plants, and locations is:						
13. Statements in the bylaws and resolutions of the Board governing the conduct of individual board members with respect to attendance at meetings, conflicts of interest, term of service and retirement, use of confidential information, annual disclosure to other board members of changes in occupation or professional and financial connection are:						
Performance of the Board						
1. Performance of the Board in formulating short—and long—run goals for the institution is:						
2. The Board's ability to monitor its own accomplishments and progress is:						
3. The performance of the Board in achieving objectives:						
Set one year ago is:						
Set three years ago is:						
4. Standards of performance expected by the Board for:						
The several parts of the institution are:						
The institution as a whole are:						
5. Standards used by the Board to measure performance by:						
Individual parts of the institution are:						
The institution as a whole are:						
6. Ability of the Board to measure the progress of the president toward achieving institutional objectives is:						
7. Ability of the Board to acquire external, objective opinion regarding the institution's progress is:						
8. Cooperation among board members and ability of the Board to act as a team is:						

Board Self-Rating Schedule	Excellent	Good	Fair	Poor	Non-existent	No Opinion
Committees						
1. Bylaw provisions or resolutions of the Board stating functions, duties, and limits of authority of committees are:						
For the Executive Committee:						
For the Program Committee:						
For the Audit Committee:						
For the Property Committee:						
For the Finance Committee:						
For the other committees: (as appropriate to the institution)						
2. Form of committee reports is:						
Method of receiving, approving or amending, and recording reports is:						
Board Meetings						
1. Format of the agenda for board meetings is:						
2. Extent to which board members do their "homework" and are prepared for meetings is:						
3. Quality of discussion at meetings is:						
4. The division of time at meetings between routine matters of the institution and long-range planning is:						
5. The division of time at meetings between day-to-day matters of the institution and long-range planning is:						
Relations with Management						
1. Understanding of the areas reserved for board decisions is:						
2. Distinctions between board business and administrative, professional or staff functions are:						
3. The Board's working relations with:						
Administrators are:						
Staff are:						
Professionals are:						
Other constituencies (as appropriate to the institution) are:						

Part III

Appendixes

Appendix A

For Voluntary Organizations in Trouble— Or Don't Want To Be *

After years of observing and trying to help organizations in trouble, I've gradually learned to diagnose some of the danger signs and want to help volunteer and staff leaders avoid or face up to them.

From the opposite side, I've spent as many years marveling at organizations that are models of effectiveness and am finally able to understand and interpret why they are so good.

This piece draws on both experiences, to assist organizations that are in trouble or don't want to be, and to try to give a boost to all those that aspire to be the best.

---

*This piece appeared originally as an INDEPENDENT SECTOR pamphlet (1993) still available from IS. Many of the observations and recommendations in this piece appear in earlier parts of this edition of *The Board Member's Book*, but because many people have said it's helpful to have these warning signs in summary form, I've left the contents substantially intact.

Danger Signs of Organizations in Trouble

When I'm asked to meet with the board or leaders of a nonprofit organization that describes itself as in trouble, the difficulty invariably relates to one or more of these "at risk" stages or weaknesses.

Failure to Focus on Mission and Priorities

One of the first things I do when meeting with a board that is confused, troubled, or divided is to ask them to complete this sentence, "The mission of this organization is. . . ." At that stage, I ask them not to discuss it or to opt out of the assignment but to write down their interpretation as best they can.

When those slips are turned in, I ask someone to put them on larger sheets of paper, and while this is taking place, I ask the board members to finish this sentence, "The single most important thing the organization should accomplish this year is. . . ." Again, I ask for no discussion or opting out. These answers are also transferred to larger sheets, and then both sets are put up on the wall.

And then I don't say a word.

For minutes, people will look over the mission statements and interpretations of priority activities and finally someone is almost certain to say something like, "No wonder we're so mixed up!"

Ninety percent of the time when organizations are in trouble the difficulty includes a failure to understand or focus on the mission and primary activities.

Failure to Invest in Building the Board

For the head of the board, having enthusiastic and reliable board members is almost as good as having an enthusiastic spouse and reliable children—and some days, such as just before the annual board meeting, you might trade the kids 2 for 1. The problem is that most of us wait until those moments of crisis to give adequate consideration to solid board membership. It's like trying to build a professional football team without the efforts of scouting, signing, training, and rewarding. Our business is almost entirely people related, yet we invest almost nothing in people building. We get so tied up in today's needs that we don't reserve a realistic part of our resources for developing the talent and dedication necessary to carry and expand the association's efforts tomorrow. The building begins with the board itself.

Executive directors, board chairpersons, and directors will go on at length that the board doesn't include enough dedicated people, diversity, fundraisers, and on and on, but when I inquire about the amount of effort invested in cultivating such people, the truth is it's almost nil.

Sometimes the neglect is rationalized on the basis that every possible resource has to be invested in the program of the organization, but I counter fairly strongly that the program is hardly protected or advanced if the board is not functioning effectively.

Lack of Funds

If there is any one problem highlighted by organizations in trouble, it's lack of funds and fundraising capacity. Almost always, the groups will point out that they are at least as deserving as other causes that are doing better, but that somehow they just have not been able to attract the support or the people capable of getting it. The fundraising commitment must begin with the board and must be high on the agenda of a significant number of the trustees. Not only must it be of high priority, it must also be high in status and recognition within the organization. That's not easy. If you're wondering how to get moving, you probably already know the problem of a board of directors not really recruited with fundraising responsibilities distinctly in mind; and if you are already getting most of your support from fees, contracts, or United Way, it's even harder to stir up real fundraising interest and urgency. Raising money takes dogged persistence, bullheadedness, salesmanship, year-round cultivation, board support and encouragement, a plan, an attainable goal, and lots of excitement—to whit it's hard work. But if the board decides it's going to raise money and is willing to allocate at least 20 percent of its energy and resources to accomplish this goal, you can and will succeed.

Every time I'm asked by a board delegation if I think their organization can raise money, I repeat that they're in for some awfully hard work. I don't say this to discourage them. Indeed, I hope they'll push on, and I hope this applies to you. But if you're timid or your organization isn't really determined, you won't survive the obstacles, heartaches, and difficulties which unfortunately I can promise you are ahead. On the other hand, if you have a cause that deserves support and if you're willing to scratch, kick, and beg, you can raise money.

In recent years of enormous financial crisis for many voluntary organizations, I've met with at least 75 board and staff delegations seeking advice on development. I start with the same encouragement, but I also follow up quickly with how much work is in store. I underscore that their organization must be prepared to devote at least 20 percent of its resources to fundraising and that the board head and chief staff officer will have to devote closer to fifty percent of their time for the first year or two. The reaction is rarely, "If that's what it's going to take, we'll do it!" Usually, the reaction is that it's unrealistic for an organization to devote that much time to fundraising. I'm sorry, but the reality is that to get started or to reach a much higher level that's what it takes. Stewardship is as much about building the capacity of the organization as it is allocating those resources wisely.

Confusion Between the Role of Board and Role of Staff

I've observed that most organizations go into a temporary downturn when staff is first hired. The pattern is fairly typical. A wonderful group of dedicated volunteers, through their own individual efforts and without staff backup, have scrambled their way to having a significant program and are now at the point where they need and can afford some staff assistance. They hire a person and immediately the volunteers relax, turning much of the work over to the staff director. The volunteers assume the agency will be able to leap forward.

In about a year, or at the most two, the volunteers begin to view the scene with bewilderment; they find that the agency is doing less than it was before they hired staff and has lost much of its visibility and vitality. The volunteers will conclude that obviously the wrong staff was hired because more was being accomplished when the volunteers were doing it by themselves. Before the downturn and discouragement become irreversible, the group's members may finally realize that they turned over far too much of the job to the staff and retreated to occasional approvals of what the staff did, along with some irregular assistance to the poor bloke who is chairperson but who has begun feeling less and less responsible for the operation.

The worst illusion ever perpetrated in the nonprofit field is that the board of directors makes policy and staff carries it out. This is just not so. A board with the help of the staff makes policy and the board with the help of the staff carries it out. Unless volunteers are committed and involved in the action phase of the organization, the agency cannot develop, and in fact, should not be characterized as a voluntary organization. The staff exists to help the volunteers do the work of the organization. Staff members should not be expected or allowed to do most jobs directly. The greatest sinner is often the chairperson who gives over his or her responsibility to the executive director.

Deficits

An interesting list of objectives for good boards was described by Michael Davis of the Rosenwald Fund. One of his best was, "Face budgets with courage, endowments with doubt, deficits with dismay, and recover quickly from a surplus."

It's easy to get carried away with unduly optimistic income projections and unrealistic expectations, but resulting deficits and the horror of budget cutbacks, particularly those which involve personnel, should teach the lesson that it is better to face reality and disappointment during the budgeting process than later.

Income projections should be based on very practical and objective analysis of *current* sources of income, including a source-by-source and gift-by-gift review. This not only makes for practical budgeting but also provides sensible preparation for the degree of work necessary to renew gifts and grants and to find new money. It's essential not to anticipate substantial new income, or at least count on it, to cover fixed expenses. The usual approach for a nonprofit agency is to hope so desperately for new income that it gets counted in the budget; then, when it doesn't materialize, the group ends up with a deficit or horrendous cutback. The wiser approach is to have an opportunity for budget revisions during the year and/or allow additions according to new income actually produced.

The full board should be involved in approving the annual budget and should take this responsibility *very* seriously. Deficits are hell for everybody.

Confusion Between the Roles of the Chief Volunteer Officer and Chief Staff Officer

In troubled organizations, I often find confusion, leading to strain and alienation between the chief volunteer and chief staff officers. Organizations are particularly at risk when one of these two people leaves. Some chairpersons come from business backgrounds and might tend to leave everything to staff, weakening the chair and the board. The next time around the new chairperson might come from an organization like the League of Women Voters, which often does not have staff and therefore the volunteer leaders do it all and that board head may inadvertently take over the role of executive director. The problem today is compounded by the use of the term "chief executive officer" to describe either of the two positions, usually the staff director, but this title and the corporate model it represents rarely fit a vibrant voluntary organization.

I don't even use the term *chief executive*. It just doesn't describe the unique roles and relationships of chief volunteer and chief staff officers in a voluntary organization. The former must be active and effective, particularly in building the volunteer side of the organization. Committee heads, project chairpersons, and other officers are the chief volunteer officer's subordinates. They want to know what he or she thinks. They want to know where that person is going, and they want to know what she or he considers important to be done.

Most chairpersons assume that this kind of contact just happens; that the executive has somehow communicated all these things; that a past chairperson has oriented a successor; or even that a person, simply by having been a member of the board, grasps new and larger responsibilities. There can't be cohesion in the organization without the chairperson's involvement in orientation and training and without his or her giving a great deal of thought as to how to effectively motivate, inspire, and stimulate persons who will be carrying the major part of the load.

A great deal of time and effort needs to be invested in being sure that this unique team of chief volunteer and chief staff officers understands and respects each other's roles and is working effectively together.

Confusion About the Role of Chief Volunteer Officer

Though this may seem to have been covered above, I give it special consideration because troubled organizations are often led, and poorly so, by people who don't really understand the role of the chairperson in building a sense of teamwork and confidence throughout the organization.

Several years ago, one of my nominating committees recognized that a particular individual was the most deserving for selection as chief volunteer officer, but they were not going to select him because he was an absolute tiger in expressing opinions and putting other people down. The current chairperson felt that, if the deserving individual really understood the difference between being an aggressive board member and being the chairperson, the situation would change, and he agreed to provide orientation and mentoring for the individual if nominated. I never saw such a difference in performance. Instead of having a strong opinion on everything and expressing it stridently, the individual became a builder of confidence and people and turned out to be an absolutely first-rate leader. He acknowledged later that the difference was that he had never really thought about the job description; once he did he realized that he would have to behave very differently to succeed at it.

Confusion Between the Trusteeship Role of Board Members and Their Other Volunteer Roles

I've seen it happen repeatedly that board members and therefore staff will be terribly off balance because trustees don't feel sufficiently involved or are involved excessively in the wrong things. Gradually, I've learned that because volunteers are necessarily and appropriately involved in many of the day-to-day activities of the organization, including fundraising, annual meetings, program projects, and much more, it's understandable that at the board table they are not clear when they are functioning as trustees and when they are wearing their more general volunteer hats.

It's absolutely essential that the directors function quite literally as the trustees on matters of budgets, audits, evaluations, formal plans, hiring the executive director, and assessing performance, but these governance functions are usually only a relatively small part of a board meeting. Much of the time they are not sitting as trustees but rather sitting as interested volunteers helping think through public relations strategies, building annual meeting attendance, or assessing the effectiveness of a special event.

In these matters, the boards, out of enthusiasm and concern, tend to function as extensions of committees and staff, but because they are at the board table, they tend to make motions and decisions that seriously confuse who does what in the organization. It's inevitable that interested volunteer board members will become involved in such discussions. To try to make clear when the trustees are functioning in a governance role and when they are functioning as informed, but still informal, advisers to committees and staff, board agendas should be divided into governance matters that require trustee discussion and action and other matters on which the board members might wish to provide opinions or be informed.

I've always been fascinated how quickly serious problems within boards are dissipated when the distinction becomes clear between the trustee role of board members and their other volunteer functions.

The Problem of Trustees Who are Single-Issue Advocates or at Least Not Trustees of the Whole Organization

Many boards tend to become divided when board members feel that they are champions of various parts of the organization, such as the research or library function, and woe to anybody who challenges that particular aspect of the association's work. It's natural that board members might have a special interest in and even responsibility for parts of the organization, but it's essential that they be reminded of and function in their role as trustees responsible for the overall health of the organization.

I consulted recently with one of the largest voluntary organizations in the country and found their board operating almost as a collection of armed camps with almost no one worrying about the good of the organization as a whole. Part of the solution was to add some at-large board members whose charge, at least for the first few years, will be to make certain that all directors are constantly reminded of their larger responsibility.

Boards and Staff Who Don't Know How to Deal With Dissent or Are Protected From It

Sometimes the problem isn't contention but a lack of disagreement. In these organizations, things are ground into absolute mush before any action is taken, and any difference of opinion seems to threaten the organization's ability to function.

Don't be afraid of healthy controversy in boards and committees. If the cause is important, people will feel strongly about it, but not always in the same way. Let people debate, and even argue, but keep it within the bounds and context of the organization's meeting. Don't be too quick to refer the issue to a committee or try to mask very real differences.

Be sure that the board or committee is advised in advance, with all the necessary resource material, of items to be voted on. Try to be certain that the first time the issue comes forward the board has a chance to react and discuss it without being expected to take action. When the matter does come back, it will probably have profited from the board's discussion, and the board will not feel pushed into making premature decisions.

Once the board has acted, even by split vote, the pattern should be to move to the next item with the losers accepting that they had a fair chance to express their contrary opinion and vote. This is one of the key roles the chairperson should play in building the board team.

Organizations That Don't Evaluate Their Effectiveness, Adherence to Mission, Program Plan, and Priorities

Voluntary organizations are usually so busy doing that there isn't time, or it seems a poor use of time, to become involved with serious evaluation. Eventually, that will lead any organization into difficulty.

A medical researcher friend of mine, long active in voluntary organizations, has this wonderful description of how nonprofit groups generally evaluate their results: "Any group as bright as we are which has worked as long and hard as we have must have done a lot of good."

Evaluation doesn't have to be complicated. It can be as basic as deciding what you want to achieve by the end of the year and then figuring out later if you got there. At its simplest, evaluation starts with an attainable goal to be accomplished at a realistic date, with a prior commitment to stop what you're doing on that date to see if your goal was actually achieved. The reason so many organizations don't follow this simple procedure is that they don't even start with a plan; therefore, they don't have a specific goal or deadline to check on. The formula is that fuzzy goals equal fuzzy evaluation, and unfortunately, the combination usually adds up to fuzzy performance.

Failure to Hire the Right Executive Director

It's almost an axiom of voluntary organizations that the largest single task the board performs is to hire the executive director. Unfortunately, the job is very often done without anything like the investment it needs. Even when a careful job description is developed, along with identification of the type of person most likely to succeed in terms of personal attributes, skills, and experience, the search process is not really geared to screening for that kind of individual. Someone who makes a good impression is often selected without carefully checking your needs against the candidate's qualifications with prior employers and others.

It's particularly important that the outreach be very systematically pursued and that any serious candidates be interviewed and assessed using the checklist based on the job specifications and personal qualities.

I've had experience enough to predict that when this orderly method is used, boards will often end up hiring someone who would not have been their first choice if left to their own instincts. I would further guess that they would agree later that their instincts would have deceived them.

Boards That Don't Carefully Evaluate Performance of the Chief Staff Officer, Including Setting and Defending Appropriate Compensation

It too rarely happens that the board of directors or at least the executive committee reviews an executive director's performance. Such review should be based on the job description and the executive director's role to assist the board in carrying forward the association's work. Most organizations overlook the need for an annual review, and no evaluation is done until the point of brinkmanship is reached.

The performance of the executive director should be measured in relation to the job description, his or her effectiveness in working with the board to fulfill priorities, similar effectiveness in helping the board with its accountability standards, and his or her ability to contribute to expanded volunteer involvement and responsibility. The evaluation should take up a substantial part of a board meeting. I don't believe that this critical responsibility should ever be delegated to a personnel committee.

The session should not be nitpicking, but it should be thorough enough that if members have concerns about performance those issues will come out and be discussed objectively. At times, this process indirectly solves other relationship problems. A member of the board may be laboring under a misconception of the executive director's role or handling of a given situation, and once it's brought up the misunderstanding may be dispelled.

The chairperson should take time after the meeting to review the report, including items of commendation and areas for improvement. It should be a growth situation for the individual and therefore for the organization.

If the board's objective and fair evaluation of performance seems to suggest a mismatch, the executive director should be given an opportunity to make adjustments in performance, but if that isn't successful or just isn't at all likely, the board has to face up to its responsibility for termination and getting on with a search that will produce the right match.

At some point during the year, the board should also deal with the executive director's compensation, including salary and benefits. There should be a good deal of process involved, including being sure that the salary scale and benefits are competitive so that you are able to keep good people. It certainly is an "at risk" time for an organization when it loses a good chief staff officer. Board members often think of staff salaries and related expenses as overhead. Even fairly sophisticated boards become concerned if staff salaries begin to represent a high proportion of the budget. Contrary to this view, I frequently counsel boards that unless the staff salaries and other supporting expenses come above 50 percent of the budget, the agency probably is not doing a real job.

The basic program force of most citizen organizations is either: 1) the volunteers' time and energy, which moves the community toward improved attitudes and practices, or 2) the specialist staff members who provide direct service. The major cost of operating most voluntary organizations is the staff who provide day-to-day service to the volunteers or to the clients. The staff person serving a childhood mental illness committee or working to secure jobs for people with disabilities is just as legitimate a program expense as the nurse in a hospital, teacher in a school, or minister in a church. The staff is not overhead. I certainly agree that overhead should be kept as low as possible, and if the staff is spending most of its time on administrative activities, there is need for concern, but if staff time is logged on behalf of the mission of the organization, it is program money well spent.

Failure to Practice Openness and Full Disclosure

Some organizations that are functioning very well get into trouble because their funders, the public, or regulators don't know enough to make an accurate judgment. In this day and age, voluntary organizations have to practice a wide degree of openness and full disclosure so that there is no suspicion or doubt about the way the organization is functioning and no lack of access to information by which people can make fair judgments.

Voluntary organizations enjoy distinct privileges, such as tax-exemption and tax deductibility of contributions, and therefore bear a particular responsibility to fulfill the essential principle of the public's right to know. The nonprofit organization that attempts to deceive the public or withhold information may be doing everything else right (though probably not), but it will receive no credit for the good it does if public confidence is lost.

Failure to Live Up to Legal and Moral Responsibilities

The saddest situation by far for an organization and for the sector as a whole occurs when an organization is in trouble because it fails to live up to its legal and ethical responsibilities. INDEPENDENT SECTOR's report, "Ethics and the Nation's Voluntary and Philanthropic Community," stresses that ". . . the public expects the highest values and ethics to be practiced habitually in nonprofit organizations. Those who presume to serve the public good assume a larger public trust." The report adds, "When our institutions do not reflect high standards of openness, honesty and public service, our contributors and clients feel ill-served, and because our organizations depend on public goodwill and participation, if public support is eroded, so is our capacity for public service."

The primary level of ethical behavior relates to obeying laws, such as being sure that required reports are submitted to government. However, most expectations are of a higher order, such as being sure the contributor's dollars go as far as possible for the client and cause. An organization must have processes by which it can decide if the law is being obeyed, if thoughtful ethics are being practiced, and if tough ethical dilemmas are being openly considered and decided. Organizations that routinely utilize ethical decision-making practices will be much better prepared to handle a crisis when it hits.

INDEPENDENT SECTOR recommends that organizations have a code of ethics and that the board should take time at least annually to examine whether the code is being practiced.

The INDEPENDENT SECTOR report concludes, "Your organization should also do everything possible to be certain that the documents and the values they reflect become part of the culture of the total organization. For example, orientation sessions for new board members, staff, and volunteers should include review of the code and other documents related to values, standards, and ethical practices. All of these steps to develop and evaluate ethical practices should be seen as affirming the good an organization does and helping those involved with it to be proud of what they do."

Models of Effectiveness

In the beginning of this piece, I mentioned that though the emphasis is on avoiding trouble, it is helpful to be aware of models of effectiveness and excellence. For five years, INDEPENDENT SECTOR engaged in a large project designed to o determine the characteristics of organizations that clients, funders, boards, peers, and others consider models of excellence. The results of that project are in a book, *PROFILES OF EXCELLENCE: Studies of Effectiveness of Nonprofit Organizations*, authored by the project directors, E. B. Knauft, Renee Berger, and Sandra T. Gray, and published by Jossey-Bass. The authors summarized their findings:

> Picture a professional orchestra. Its musicians read notes proficiently, play their instruments well and practice long hours together. But it takes much more to turn a credible group of music makers into a world-class symphony orchestra.
>
> The same is true for a nonprofit organization. It takes more than a good board, a competent director and solid financial controls to differentiate the truly great organization from the larger universe of merely good ones. Our hallmarks of excellence are not substitutes for sound management practices. Rather, they are the something extra that makes all the difference.
>
> Four overarching characteristics appear repeatedly in the best nonprofit organizations. These hallmarks [of excellence] reflect more than sound management practices, good staff and effective programs—although all are important components of excellence. But the very best groups consistently manifest something more—a clear and tangible *value added*.
>
> The hallmarks of excellence in nonprofit organizations are:
>
> 1. A clearly articulated sense of mission that serves as the focal point of commitment for board and staff and is the guidepost by which the organization judges its success and makes adjustments in course over time;
> 2. An individual who truly leads the organization and creates a culture that enables and motivates the organization to fulfill its mission;
> 3. An involved and committed volunteer board that relates dynamically with the chief staff officer and provides a bridge to the larger community;
> 4. An ongoing capacity to attract sufficient financial and human resources.

The book examines in detail each of these "hallmarks" and provides case studies of organizations that became excellent by achieving them.

One quick way to look at your organization might be to match yours against a profile I developed after years of trying to figure out why some voluntary organizations fail and others succeed. The successful ones have these characteristics:

- A cause worth getting excited about.

- An ability to generate funds to do the job.

- Programs that in fact do something for the cause.

- Adequate attention to morale in order to keep the undertaking spirited and vigorous even when the immediate tasks are not.

- Appropriate emphasis on increasing the number of citizens involved.

- Ability to keep the volunteers in charge even after the operation is staffed.

- Flexibility to respond effectively to new problems and opportunities and to fit the profile of "ad-hocracy," which must increasingly characterize the useful organization.

- A capacity to keep the real mission in focus no matter how frenzied things become or how great the pressure to move into new areas. This means that all important decisions are made with the organization's "reason for being" kept clearly in the forefront.

- Vision to see beyond the horizon, along with a sensitivity to human needs and an almost contradictory toughness to build an organization capable of translating the vision and sensitivity into change.

Whether you're trying to get your organization out of trouble, avoid it, or move toward excellence, keep in mind that those who struggle on behalf of important causes open ourselves to frustration and disappointment, but through it all and after it all, those times of making things happen for the better are among our lasting joys. Hang in there.

Appendix B

Standards for Charitable Accountability of the BBB Wise Giving Alliance (2002) *

Governance and Oversight

The *governing board has the ultimate oversight authority for any charitable organization. This section of the standards seeks to ensure that the volunteer board is active, independent, and free of self-dealing. To meet these standards, the organization shall have:*

1. **A board of directors that provides adequate oversight of the charity's operations and its staff.** Indication of adequate oversight includes, but is not limited to: regularly scheduled appraisals of the CEO's performance, evidence of disbursement controls such as board approval of the budget, fundraising practices, establishment of a conflict of interest policy, and establishment of accounting procedures sufficient to safeguard charity finances.

---

*"Standards for Charitable Activity" reprinted by permission. Copyright 2002, BBB Wise Giving Alliance, 4200 Wilson Blvd., Suite 800, Arlington, VA 22203, tel. 703-276-0100, fax 703-525-8277, www.give.org.

2. A board of directors with a minimum of five voting members.

3. **A minimum of three evenly spaced meetings per year of the full governing body with a majority in attendance, with face-to-face participation.** A conference call of the full board can substitute for one of the three meetings of the governing body. For all meetings, alternative modes of participation are acceptable for those with physical disabilities.

4. **Not more than one or 10% (whichever is greater) directly or indirectly compensated person(s) serving as voting member(s) of the board. Compensated members shall not serve as the board's chair or treasurer.**

5. **No transaction(s) in which any board or staff members have material conflicting interests with the charity resulting from any relationship or business affiliation.** Factors that will be considered when concluding whether or not a related party transaction constitutes a conflict of interest and if such a conflict is material, include, but are not limited to: any arm's length procedures established by the charity; the size of the transaction relative to like expenses of the charity; whether the interested party participated in the board vote on the transaction; if competitive bids were sought and whether the transaction is one-time, recurring, or ongoing.

Measuring Effectiveness

An organization should regularly assess its effectiveness in achieving its mission. This section seeks to ensure that an organization has a defined process in place to evaluate the success and impact of its program(s) in fulfilling the goals of the organization and that also identifies ways to address any deficiencies. To meet these standards, a charitable organization shall:

6. **Have a board policy of assessing, no less than every two years, the organization's performance and of determining future actions required to achieve its mission.**

7. Submit to the organization's governing body, for its approval, a written report that outlines the results of the aforementioned effectiveness assessment and recommendations for future actions.

Finances

This section of the standards seeks to ensure that the charity spends its funds honestly, prudently and in accordance with statements made in fundraising appeals. To meet these standards, the charitable organization shall:

8. Spend at least 65% of its <u>total expenses</u> on program activities.

> Formula for Standard 8:
>
> $$\frac{\text{Total program Service Expenses}}{\text{Total Expenses}} \quad \text{Should be at least } 65\%$$

9. Spend no more than 35% of <u>related contributions</u> on fundraising.

   Related contributions includes donations, legacies, and other gifts received as a result of fundraising efforts.

> Formula for Standard 9:
>
> $$\frac{\text{Total Fundraising Expenses}}{\text{Total Related Contributions}} \quad \text{Should be less than } 35\%$$

> Please note: Standards 8 and 9 have <u>different</u> denominators.

10. Avoid accumulating funds that could be used for current program activities. To meet this standard, the charity's unrestricted net assets available for use should not be more than three times the size of the past year's expenses or three times the size of the current year's budget, whichever is higher.

An organization that does not meet Standards 8, 9, and/or 10 may provide evidence to demonstrate that its use of funds is reasonable. The higher fundraising and administrative costs of a newly created organization, donor restrictions on the use of funds, exceptional bequests, a stigma associated with a cause, and environmental or political events beyond an organization's control are among factors which may result in expenditures that are reasonable although they do not meet the financial measures cited in these standards.

11. Make available to all, on request, complete annual financial statements prepared in accordance with generally accepted accounting principles. When total annual gross income exceeds $250,000, these statements should be audited in accordance with generally accepted auditing standards. For charities whose annual gross income is less than $250,000, a review by a certified public accountant is sufficient to meet this standard. For charities whose annual gross income is less than $100,000, an internally produced, complete financial statement is sufficient to meet this standard.

12. Include in the financial statements a breakdown of expenses (e.g., salaries, travel, postage, etc.) that shows what portion of these expenses was allocated to program, fundraising, and administrative activities. If the charity has more than one major program category, the schedule should provide a breakdown for each category.

13. Accurately report the charity's expenses, including any joint cost allocations, in its financial statements. For example, audited or unaudited statements which inaccurately claim zero fundraising expenses or otherwise understate the amount a charity spends on fundraising, and/or overstate the amount it spends on programs will not meet this standard.

14. Have a board-approved annual budget for its current fiscal year, outlining projected expenses for major program activities, fundraising, and administration.

Fundraising and Informational Materials

A *fundraising appeal is often the only direct contact a donor has with a charity and may be the sole impetus for giving. This section of the standards seeks to ensure that a charity's representations to the public are accurate, complete, and respectful. To meet these standards, the charitable organization shall:*

15. **Have solicitations and information materials, distributed by any means, that are accurate, truthful and not misleading, both in whole and in part.** Appeals that omit a clear description of program(s) for which contributions are sought will not meet this standard. A charity should also be able to substantiate that the timing and nature of its expenditures are in accordance with what is stated, expressed, or implied in the charity's solicitations.

16. **Have an annual report, available on request to all, that includes:**

     (a) the organization's mission statement,

     (b) a summary of the past year's program service accomplishments,

     (c) a roster of the officers and members of the board of directors,

     (d) financial information that includes: (i) total income in the past fiscal year, (ii) expenses in the same program, fundraising, and administrative categories as in the financial statements, and (iii) ending net assets.

17. Include on any charity web sites that solicit contributions, the same information that is recommended for annual reports, as well as the mailing address of the charity and electronic access to its most recent IRS Form 990.

18. Address privacy concerns of donors by:

(a) providing, in written appeals, at least annually, a means (e.g., such as a check off box) for both new and continuing donors to inform the charity if they do not want their name and address shared outside the organization, and

(B) providing a clear, prominent, and easily accessible privacy policy on any of its web sites that tells visitors: (i) what information, if any, is being collected about them by the charity and how this information will be used, (ii) how to contact the charity (e.g., a check off box) that the visitor does not wish his/her personal information to be shared outside the organization, and (iii) what security measures the charity has in place to protect personal information.

19. Clearly disclose how the charity benefits from the sale of products or services (i.e., cause-related marketing) that state or imply that a charity will benefit from a consumer sale or transaction. Such promotions should disclose, at the point of solicitation:

(a) the actual or anticipated portion of the purchase price that will benefit the charity (e.g., 5 cents will be contributed to abc charity for every xyz company product sold),

(b) the duration of the campaign (e.g., the month of October),

(c) any maximum or guaranteed minimum contribution amount (e.g., up to a maximum of $200,000).

20. Respond promptly to and act on complaints brought to its attention by the BBB Wise Giving Alliance and/or local Better Business Bureaus about fundraising practices, privacy policy violations, and/or other issues.

Appendix C

Robert's Rules of Order— Demystified

Robert's *Rules of Order* can be very complicated—but almost always unnecessarily. Occasionally all that complexity is required—and that's why the Rules are extensive—but for most of us, it comes down to some fairly simple ground rules that in turn are based on common sense and courtesy. These will get you through 99 percent of the situations you are likely to face.

Robert's Rules of Order begins with this basic rule of fairness: "American Parliamentary Law is built upon the principle that rights must be respected: rights of the majority, of the minority, of individuals, of absentees, and rights of all of these together."

There's one quick way you can be smarter about *Robert's Rules* than almost anybody else. You are about to become one of the rare ones who knows who Robert was! Poor Robert almost always gets left out, even by the show-offs who can recite which divided motions can't be amended. The next time one of them tries to bamboozle you with more knowledge than common sense, get him or her aside and casually ask who Robert was? Chances are, that will be one up for you.

Robert was Henry Martin Robert, a young Civil War officer on the Union side, who later became a general and head of the Washington, D.C., District. He took on the task of codifying and simplifying the rules of procedure of the U.S. House of Representatives. The work was completed in 1876, at which time General Robert adapted those rules to fit other civic organizations.

Other rule books have been written, but *Robert's* is still the basic text. Indeed, if your own bylaws or rules don't stipulate otherwise, it is standard practice, and the law in many states, that *Robert's Rules* shall be used in the resolution of internal differences.

I'll begin with the most common parliamentary procedures you are likely to need. Indeed, once you are a third of the way through this review, you'll have covered most of what you'll ever need to know and probably more than you want to know.

Starting at the most elementary level, this is the way a group formally makes a decision:

- One of the members will *move* that a decision be made (this is proposing that the board go on record in favor of a certain definite action).

- Another member of the group will *second* the motion, which means "support" for the action proposed. (The second is necessary to be certain that the issue is of interest to more than one person.)

- Once the motion has been made and seconded, there is *discussion, clarification, and debate.*

- When the subject has been covered fully, there is the *vote.*

- Prior to both discussion and vote, the person in the chair should *restate the motion* to be certain everyone knows what is being discussed and decided.

It may strike you as an enormous simplification, but for most committees and boards, that's all you need to know: a motion, second, discussion, and vote.

The next level involves a situation in which the group considers that it might want to make some changes in the motion as originally offered. In the course of the discussion, it may become obvious that the motion doesn't quite say what the board now has in mind. This is the way that a slightly more complicated scenario would unfold:

- The motion.

- The second.

- The chairperson restates the motion.

- Discussion, clarification, and debate.

- Someone suggests that the original motion be amended, and another person seconds the idea. (At that point it will usually happen that the maker and seconder of the original or main motion will agree to the amendment even though a vote on the amendment has not been taken. Technically, once a motion has been made and seconded, it involves the whole assembly, but if no one offers objection to the amendment, no vote is usually taken.)

- If the persons who moved and seconded the original motion do not agree to the amendment or anyone else voices objection, then there is discussion, clarification, and debate on the amendment itself.

- After the group has adequately considered the amendment, the chairperson restates the motion to amend, and the group *votes on the amendment.*

- Once the amendment has been accepted or rejected, the group returns its attention to the original motion.

- If the amendment passed, the main motion would now be known as "the original motion as amended." If the amendment had been defeated, it would simply be "the original motion."

- Debate would proceed on the original motion. It could be amended again, in which case it would be the new amendment that gets the informal or formal consideration.

- When the amendments have been disposed of, the board votes on the original motion (as amended, if that's the case). Although that is slightly more complicated, it is simply the group's way of deciding whether the original motion needed some changes before it reflected the combined view of what should be done.

- If the main motion is defeated, the same basic proposal cannot be brought forward again at the same meeting. That's to keep the losers from filibustering by bringing the same motion up again and again. (There is an exception. If one person who was on the winning side of the vote realizes that he or she may have made a mistake, such as misunderstanding what the motion called for, he or she can move for reconsideration, at which point the board decides whether to allow reconsideration.)

If you serve on a fairly informal board or committee that rarely gets involved in parliamentary procedure, don't bother with the rest of this chapter. For those who participate in more involved board deliberations, including debates, there are some additional points worth knowing.

(1) As obvious as it may be, it is important to know that if a motion is made and *not seconded*, the motion is automatically lost, and nothing further should be said about it. If there isn't a second, it means that the subject is not something the group wants to spend time on, and the individual who proposed the motion should not presume upon the group's good nature by commenting on the subject as though it had been accepted for discussion ("on the table").

(2) Almost all motions can have only two amendments to them before a vote must be taken on at least one of those amendments. Otherwise everyone would get lost, and the main motion would be obscured. For example, if the original motion and second call for spending $2,000 for new chairs around the conference table, one amendment may suggest changing the amount to $3,000, and a subsequent and separate amendment may propose that the money be spent for chairs and a new conference table. If any more amendments were allowed, you can see how people would get confused about what they are expected to decide.

Also, amendments must be "germane," that is, they must relate to the subject of the motion that would be amended. You can't have an amendment that introduces a different issue.

(3) A motion to amend can also be the subject of a motion to amend ("I move that the amendment be amended"), but there can be only one such motion to amend an amendment on the floor at any one time.

The debate and vote would first apply to the motion to amend the amendment. After that is disposed of, there can be fuller discussion and the vote on the amendment, and finally additional discussion and vote on the original motion (as amended, if the amendment was approved).

At the risk of laboring the point, let me provide a recap in the form of an example:

- "I move that we have a fundraising dinner and do it in June."

- "I second the motion."

- "We have a motion before us to have a fundraising dinner and do it in June. The floor is open for discussion."

- Discussion.

- An amendment: "I like the idea, but I wonder if we should tie the hands of the committee by stipulating June. Would the maker and seconder of the motion be willing to delete that reference to the month of June?"

- The maker and seconder may accept the deletion, and if no one else offers objection, discussion would proceed on the original motion without the reference to June.

- The maker and/or the seconder of the original motion or anyone else may not agree to the deletion and therefore not accept the amendment. ("I like parties in June," he exclaimed!) In that case, if the person offering the amendment feels strongly enough about the issue to want a formal consideration of his or her idea, a motion would be made to amend the original motion by deleting the phrase "and do it in June."

- The amendment would require a second.

- The chairperson would state the motion to amend.

- Discussion, clarification, and debate would proceed *on the amendment.*

- After ample discussion, there would be a vote on the amendment; let's assume that the amendment "to delete June" passes. ("I hate you!" shouts the maker of the original motion. Sometimes even *Robert's Rules* don't assure courtesy!)

- After the vote on the amendment, the group returns to a discussion of the original motion.

- After ample consideration, the group votes on the original or main motion.

The amendment to "delete June" could have been amended if someone else had moved, "O.K. Let's not specify June, but let's stipulate that it has to be done sometime between April and July." ("How about the last day in May or any time in June?" pleads the originator, but the chairperson gavels him out of order.)

Usually the maker and seconder of the amendment and everyone else present will accept that kind of change without challenge, and discussion and vote would proceed upon the original amendment. If they don't informally accept the change to the amendment, then the immediate discussion and vote are on the substitution of the phrase "sometime between April and July" in place of the phrase "and do it in June."

Once the substitution has been discussed and voted on, the group would return to a discussion and a vote on the amendment. In cases such as this, the vote on the amendment to the amendment nullifies the need for the amendment itself. If the group has voted to hold the event "sometime between April and July," there's no need to vote on the "to delete June" issue. If, however, the amendment to the amendment lost, then it would be necessary to vote on the amendment "to delete June."

After the first amendment has been dealt with, the group would again return to discussion and consideration of the main motion.

By this point in my explanation, parliamentarians are probably on their feet hollering that I must explain the difference between "amendment" and "substitution," which I'll do at the end of this lesson.

(4) For most votes, a majority of those present is all that's needed to approve or disapprove a motion. (This is called a "simple majority.")

Your bylaws and *Robert's Rules* may stipulate that certain votes require a two-thirds majority, such as for amendment of the bylaws (or impeachment of the president, who by this point would recognize any seconder).

A two-thirds majority is also required to suspend the rules, close nominations, or end debate.

(5) You'll frequently hear people say, "I move the previous question," or, "Move the question," or even "Question."

When a member of the board feels that discussion has gone on long enough, he or she can move that debate be ended—in essence saying, "I move that debate be ended and that we now vote immediately on the motion before us." The motion before the group can be an amendment to an amendment or the original motion. Calling for an end to debate is usually referred to as "the previous question."

If there is a second, there can be no debate on the motion to close debate, but two-thirds of the group must vote for the motion. If they do, there must be an immediate vote on the issue at hand. If "the previous question" is not approved, debate on the issue at hand proceeds. After an interval, someone else can also move the previous question, but if the group doesn't feel that all the points or people they want to hear have been heard—or if they are not sick of the topic—they can again defeat the "question."

There is a pervasive misperception about "the previous question." Frequently one or more people will feel that the group is ready for a vote and will say "Question" or "Move the question." Then the person in the chair will assume that the group must therefore vote and will cut off further debate. Debate cannot be ended unless the group actually agrees.

The person in the chair can say something like, "Some people are ready to vote—does the whole group agree." If just one person disagrees or is waiting to say something, the debate continues. If those who called "Question" really mean it, they must formally move the previous question and see if two-thirds of the group agree to end debate.

The maker of the motion being debated can't propose ending debate. Be alert also for those who have already had their say who want to deny the same chance to others.

When someone shouts "Question!" it's appropriate for the chairperson to say, "I know several people still seem to want to speak to the issue and as a matter of fairness I will let the discussion proceed." If someone formally moves the previous questions, even the person in the chair can't do any more than clarify what the group is voting on (closing debate) and that it requires a two-thirds vote.

(6) Some other motions are not debatable:

- "Protest a breach of rules or conduct." *("She's pulling my hair.")*

- "Call for intermission." *("With all this coffee, doesn't anyone else need to. . . ?")*

- "Complain about conditions." *("This heat is so bad, my underwear is sticking!")*

- "Avoid considering an improper matter." *("I agree we should all be concerned about fluoridation, but after all, this is an association of grandmothers for planned parenthood!")*

- "Confirm a decision by calling for a standing vote." *("I know it sounded unanimous, but with this crazy person in the chair, it's the only way we're ever going to get to stretch.")*

- "Call for a point of information." (*"Are you out of your cotton-pickin' mind!?"*)

(7) Voting can go from the very informal to formal. The chairperson may say something like, "There appears to be a clear consensus, and unless anyone objects, we'll assume the matter is approved." If that's not challenged, it would be considered an unchallenged vote. (In the original draft of this chapter, I said that "it would be considered a unanimous vote." The Master Parliamentarian who reviewed the chapter for me said that it is incorrect to assume that silence means support. Technically then, the only votes that can be recorded as unanimous are when each person actually votes on the same side.)

Very often there is call for a voice vote: "All those in favor, please say 'Aye.' All those opposed, please say 'No.'" Usually the decision is obvious. Frequently because most people seem to have voted "Aye," there is not a call for the "No" votes. That's not good practice. It's good for the group to see that votes are unanimous or unchallenged, and it's equally important that people have a chance to register their dissent.

If the results of the voice vote are not clear or if it's the practice of the organization to try to make a record of how people vote, then there would be a raising of the hands for "Aye" and "No." Sometimes this is done as a standing vote.

If the vote is still not clear or if it is important that there be a clear record of votes, there can be an actual roll call, with each member asked to respond "Aye" or "No." If a person prefers not to vote, he or she can just say "Present."

In large gatherings, there can be a "count off." All those in favor stand up, and the chairperson designates a person to begin. That person says "one" and sits down, the next person says "two" and is seated, and so forth until all those who were standing have counted off and been seated. Then those voting "No" go through the same procedure. This is a clear way to get an actual count and to guarantee that no one is voting twice or not being counted.

At the extreme there can be a ballot. This is sometimes used in voting on nominees or on very sensitive issues.

Any member can call for any one of these voting procedures, and it is up to the chairperson to decide. If he or she decides against such a suggestion, the group can go through the formal procedure of a motion, second, debate, and vote on whether to accept the voting procedure called for in the motion. Usually the chairperson goes along, unless it is a delaying tactic that the chairperson believes is fundamentally unfair to the group.

(8) The Motion to Table is used often enough and has enough confusion surrounding it that you may want to have some briefing about it. If a board member feels that the discussion is not getting anywhere or that the group clearly does not want to decide the issue at hand (at least at that time), the individual can "move to table." This requires a second and is not debatable. Only a majority vote is required.

The move to table is often used to "kill" the matter, but others have the privilege of bringing it up again ("take it from the table") later in the meeting or at a future meeting. To take an item "from the table" requires a motion and a second, is not debatable, and can be approved by a simple majority.

Sometimes items are postponed to "a time certain," such as, "I move that this item be postponed until after we've disposed of these other matters," or "until the next meeting," or "until the budget has been developed." A motion to postpone is debatable.

The motion to table is a more deliberate challenge to the matter at hand. Some people really don't want to deal with the issue, and they want an immediate sense of the assembly. The motion to postpone is a more practical scheduling situation.

In preparation for the annual meetings of delegates to the National Mental Health Association, we included in the advance resource packets a "Basic Chart of Motions." Those meetings frequently involved complicated subjects and charged debates; we also frequently ran into self-styled parliamentarians. We wanted everybody to be on equal footing or at least to have readily at hand a chart that explained what was going on and what their rights were.

The Channing Bete Company has produced a good primer called *The ABC's of Parliamentary Procedure* that includes "Parliamentary Procedure . . . At a Glance," which is reproduced at the end of this section. It gives a good overview of many of the basic procedures you are likely to run into.

If you're a perfectionist or a masochist, you can get your own set of *Robert's Rules of Order Newly Revised, 10th Edition*, Henry M. Robert III, William J. Evans, Daniel H. Honemann, Thomas J. Balch, New York, NY: Perseus Books Group, 2000.

For some of you it might be helpful to talk briefly about parliamentarians. Usually it's sufficient that the chairperson has some grasp of the basic rules. It's probably more important for persons who regularly staff boards and committees to be reasonably familiar with *Robert's Rules*, at least to the extent of knowing the kinds of matters covered in the "Parliamentary Procedures." I routinely recommend to staff members that one of the items in the file carried to all meetings should be a summary of parliamentary procedures.

Many organizations identify a particular board member as the informal parliamentarian. It's important to be sure that the individual in that role will be even-handed. It's equally important that the individual not get the group more deeply involved in parliamentary procedure than is necessary.

When major controversy is to be put before the board, or if certain types of meetings routinely involve very complicated or divisive matters, a professional parliamentarian should be at hand. In those cases the parliamentarian should not be a member of the board. The person chairing the meeting should do everything possible to put the issues out for full and adequate debate before the parliamentary maneuvering begins. Despite the good intentions of *Robert's Rules of Order*, their implementation often thwarts early consideration of the broad issues. Someone's always quick to jump in with a motion to amend, motion to substitute, motion to split, and all the other maneuvering that so often focuses debate either on the parliamentary procedures themselves or on issues that may not get at the heart of the matter.

For the names of qualified professional parliamentarians in your area, you can write:

National Association of Parliamentarians (NAP)
213 South Main Street
Independence, MO 64050-3850
(816) 833-3892
Website: www.parliamentarians.org

American Institute of Parliamentarians (AIP)
P.O. Box 2173
Wilmington, DE 19899-2173
(888) 664-0428 or (302) 762-1811
Website: www.parliamentaryprocedure.org

One of the best summaries of parliamentary matters I ever came across was put together by O. Garfield Jones at the University of Toledo in 1932. While giving ample attention to helping the reader work through the maze of what's possible, Jones emphasized that, ". . . common sense is the essence of parliamentary rules; fair play is their guiding principle; reasonable discussion followed by prompt action is what they are devised to achieve."

Parliamentary Procedure . . . at a Glance*

To Do This:	You Say This:	May You Interrupt the Speaker?	Do You Need a Second?	Is It Debatable?	Can It Be Amended?	What Vote Is Needed?	Can it be Reconsidered
ADJOURN MEETING	"I move to adjourn."	NO	YES	NO	NO	MAJORITY	NO
CALL AN INTERMISSION	"I move to recess for . . ."	NO	YES	NO[1]	YES	MAJORITY	NO
COMPLAIN ABOUT HEAT, NOISE, ETC.	"I rise to a question of privilege."	YES	NO	NO	NO	NO VOTE	NO
NO TEMPORARILY SUSPEND CONSIDERATION OF AN ISSUE	"I move to lay the motion on the table."	NO	YES	NO	NO	MAJORITY	NO[2]
END DEBATE AND AMENDMENTS	"I move the previous question."	NO	YES	NO	NO	2/3	YES[3]
POSTPONE DISCUSSION FOR A CERTAIN TIME	"I move to postpone the discussion until . . ."	NO	YES	YES	YES	MAJORITY	YES
GIVE CLOSER STUDY OF SOMETHING	"I move to refer the matter to committee."	NO	YES	YES	YES	MAJORITY	YES[4]
AMEND A MOTION	"I move to amend the motion by . . ."	NO	YES	YES[5]	YES	MAJORITY	YES
INTRODUCE BUSINESS	"I move that . . ."	NO	YES	YES	YES	MAJORITY	YES

THE MOTIONS LISTED ABOVE ARE IN ORDER OF PRECEDENCE . . . BELOW THERE IS NO ORDER . . .

[1] Unless vote moved when no question is pending.
[2] Affirmative votes may not be reconsidered.
[3] Unless vote on question has begun.
[4] Unless the committee has already taken up the subject.
[5] Unless the motion to be amended is not debatable.

Parliamentary Procedure . . . at a Glance*

To Do This:	You Say This:	May You Interrupt the Speaker?	Do You Need a Second?	Is It Debatable?	Can It Be Amended?	What Vote Is Needed?	Can it be Reconsidered
PROTEST BREACH OF RULES OR CONDUCT	"I rise to a point of order."	YES	NO	NO	NO	NO VOTE[6]	NO
VOTE ON A RULING OF THE CHAIR	"I appeal from the chair's decision."	YES	YES	YES	NO	MAJORITY	YES
SUSPEND RULES TEMPORARILY	"I move to suspend the rules so that . . ."	NO	YES	NO	NO	2/3	NO
AVOID CONSIDERING AN IMPROPER MATTER	"I object to consideration of this motion."	YES	NO	NO	NO	2/3[7]	YES[2]
VERIFY A VOICE VOTE BY HAVING MEMBERS STAND	"I call for a division or "Division""	YES	NO	NO	NO	NO VOTE	NO
REQUEST INFORMATION	"Point of information . . ."	YES	NO	NO	NO	NO VOTE	NO
TAKE UP A MATTER PREVIOUSLY TABLED	"I move to take from the table . . ."	YES	YES	NO	NO	MAJORITY	NO
RECONSIDER A HASTY ACTION	"I move to consider the vote on . . ."	YES[8]	YES	YES[9]	NO	MAJORITY	NO

[6] Unless the chair submits to the assembly for decision.
[7] A 2/3 vote in negative needed to prevent consideration of main motion.
[8] Only if speaker has the floor but has not actually begun to speak.
[9] Unless the motion to be reconsidered is not debatable.

Appendix D

*For The Fun of It: Minutes of Our Last Meeting**

MINUTES OF OUR LAST MEETING

Association Office
October 26, 2002

PRESENT
Rodney Russell, Chairperson
Harry Gonzalez, Treasurer
Mrs. Jeffrey (Effi) Black, Secretary
Hon. Peter Paul Henderson, *Founder First*
    Chairperson, and Chairperson Emeritus
    (79th consecutive meeting)
Carol Archer
Louella Buckminster
George Colberg
Pat Greenlaw
Rev. Bryant Horsinger
George Horton
Bruce Knight

Harriet Lortz
Kathleen O'Reilly
Alan Cala
Joseph Shapiro
Beth Trister
Paul Widen
Lucas Zukert
Staff:
Jack Neal, Executive Secretary
Paula Masonowitz, Office Manager,
    Administrative Assistant, Assistant
    Secretary, and Assistant Treasurer

ABSENT
Penelope Mitchell, Vice Chairperson
(absent again!)

Samuel Fales
(excused for personal reasons)

---

* Since these initial "Minutes" appeared in the first edition of *The Board Member's Book* (1985), their popularity led to a separate book, *Our Organization*, which contained eight such reports of meetings of the same hapless but humorous collection of board members. *Our Organization* was published by Walker & Company, New York, NY, 1987. Subsequently, a revised edition under the title *BOARD OVERBOARD: Laughs and Lessons For All But the Perfect Nonprofit* was published by Jossey-Bass Publishers, San Francisco, CA, 1996.

Mr. Russell opened the meeting at 8:07 P.M. and immediately turned the meeting over to me, Mrs. Jeffrey (Effi) Black, Secretary of the Board of Directors, for reading of the minutes of the last meeting. I announced that copies would be distributed at the conclusion of the reading. Mr. Scala asked if they could be distributed immediately so that we might dispense with the reading. I pointed out to Mr. Scala—as I had on several previous occasions—that *Robert's Rules of Order* require a reading of the minutes. I also indicated that I had gotten out of a sick bed to fulfill this duty.

Mr. Russell suggested that we compromise by distributing the minutes in advance but still go ahead with the reading and everyone agreed. Mr. Scala, in a rare display of cooperation, complimented the chairperson for having the diplomacy to propose what he called a "Read Along." He suggested that for our next meeting we put it all to music and call it a Minute Minuet. Everyone chuckled. Mrs. Lortz said any composition as long as my minutes couldn't be called a minuet. Nobody laughed. I read the minutes.

The chairperson next called on the Treasurer to give the financial report.

Mr. Gonzalez said that income for the first six months was only $73,000, but projected receipts for the second half were $809,000. Ms. Trister asked if this was realistic, but Mr. Gonzalez pointed out that, as Treasurer, he dealt with expenses, not income. Ms. Trister apologized.

The Treasurer did say he had heard indirectly that fundraising looked terrific. George Colberg asked if this was reflected yet in the financial statements. Mr. Gonzalez asked our Executive Secretary, who said that bookkeeping was a little behind because our one-day-a-week bookkeeper-Dictaphone transcriber-telephone operator and general handy person had been on maternity leave and had just had a little boy. Everyone clapped and agreed to a resolution to send a letter of congratulations to the proud parents. A committee was appointed to select a gift.

The bookkeeping situation prompted Mr. Colberg to ask if we had an audit yet for 1999. Jack apologized, saying we still don't, but added that we have to be patient because the service is being done for free by Mrs. Workenthrader's son, who used to be an accountant but who is now in the Peace Corps and is away a lot.

Mr. Colberg asked whether Mr. Neal or Mr. Gonzalez had any general idea of what the income looked like in the three and one-half months since the June 30 statement. Jack deferred to the Treasurer, who said that, as manager of the branch where the association did it's banking, he was aware that deposits were dropping off and that the Executive Secretary had inquired what a line of credit was. Other than that, he didn't know and would have to defer to the Fundraising Chairman. Mr. Widen said he would prefer waiting to give his report until there was a more positive atmosphere.

Jack Neal said he didn't want to ignore some rough patches in our financial picture, but he could confide to the Board that he had heard from an attorney in town that the association might be getting a nice bequest. In answer to questions, Jack said he didn't know absolutely how much or how soon. This prompted Mrs. O'Reilly to ask if we knew whether the benefactor was dead yet. Jack said he had felt it was too delicate a question to ask. The Honorable Peter Paul Henderson, Founder, First Chairperson, and Chairperson Emeritus, said he would check around to see if he could find out who it was and, if still alive, whether we could hope that developments might still help our cash flow this year. Everyone expressed appreciation.

Mr. Gonzalez said that on the expense side, things looked much better—that we were only 16 percent above the same time last year. Mr. Knight said this was indeed good news, but didn't he recall that we had cut the budget by about 20 percent? The Treasurer acknowledged we had, but explained that just because a board cuts the budget, it doesn't mean that expenses go down. There was a long, thoughtful silence.

Mrs. Archer said she didn't know much about finances, but was she close to the mark in guessing that with income so far below expectations and expenses so far above budget that the picture was somewhat negative?

To get specific, Mr. Colberg asked the Treasurer how he, from a banker's perspective, would view the situation if income for the last half was only as good as the first half and if expenditures remained at their current level. Mr. Gonzalez, responding in the professional spirit in which the question was asked, replied, "Stinky."

In terms of figures, he indicated that the shortfall would be about $475,000.00 against reserves of $19,875.53. Mrs. Masonowitz, the Assistant Treasurer, asked what a line of credit was.

To put things on a more positive track, Mr. Russell asked the Fundraising Chairman to report.

Mr. Widen explained that there were some disappointments. To begin with, the Special Event with a half million dollar goal fell short. We had not been able to get Tiger Woods, Oprah Winfrey, or their backup, President Bush, and that they had to settle for Merty Pink, the first woman deejay at Station WOLP, who turned out to be less of a drawing card than hoped. The event raised $783.87. Expenses were $1,113.53. But Mr. Widen indicated that, "We got great publicity for the association, so the overall effort should be viewed as a long-term investment."

The direct-mail solicitation also came up short. Mr. Widen and his advisers had assumed that with the emotional pull our cause represents, plus the power of this Board and the success of so many less worthy mail campaigns, that we didn't need the ridiculous expense of a direct-mail firm or the loss of precious time in test marketing; so Mr. Widen had volunteered to write the letters himself and to have them reproduced on his mimeograph. He reminded the Board that he had asked all of them to take a supply home and to mail them to all their friends. As of the meeting date, all of the responses were not in, and 13 of the 24 Board members had not yet mailed theirs, but being realistic, this part of the campaign would have to be viewed as a failure. The costs so far, not including staff time, were $1,756, and income was $98, not including an "in-kind" gift by the Fundraising Chairman's own company. This gift was valued at $2,500 for reproduction, proofreading, messenger delivery, etc. Everyone thanked Mr. Widen for his personal generosity.

Actually, not everyone. Mrs. Buckminster asked Mr. Widen if the expenses included any reimbursements to his firm. Mr. Widen asked that the Chairperson rule the question out of order and rude and hurtful. Fortunately, Jack Neal stepped in to indicate that Mr. Widen had given a great party for the guys and gals in his shop and in the association, all of whom had done most of the work on the mail appeal. Mr. Neal said that this extra effort on behalf of the campaign added spirit and thrust to the 2002 Drive and, therefore, was not only in good taste but entirely within accounting standards. Besides, he said many of the hors d'oeuvres were donated.

Mr. Zukert asked what the average contribution was from the letters the board members themselves had sent out. The answer was $3.26. There was extended discussion whether this was the result of the board members not having the right friends, not having enough friends, or for the 13 who had not mailed any letters, no friends at all. After a heated exchange, it was agreed to refer the issue to the Nominating Committee.

Mr. Widen then reported on the part of the Drive involving contributions from the board members themselves. He reminded the group that it was an axiom of board membership that the board exists to provide "wisdom, work, and wealth." The Honorable Peter Paul Henderson, Founder, First Chairperson, and Chairperson Emeritus, reacted, as he had on previous occasions, by saying that he found the phrase crass and undignified. Mr. Widen indicated that it was not necessary for Mr. Henderson to remind the Board of the value of his years of service involved in founding the association and guiding it to its current level.

The advance gifts solicitation from the Board was to have been the "leadership" part of the Drive, but it was not yet under way. It has been the major subject of seven board meetings. Most recently, the Board has not been able to agree on whether there should be a suggested level or standard for contributions from the Board. This issue, in turn, has been subdivided into two issues:

1. Should the time given by board members be considered in lieu of cash?

    Mr. Russell, our Chairperson, is on record as saying that ordinarily the dollar value of volunteer time should not be considered but that in his case there should be an exception, particularly in light of how much time he is having to spend at the task. (It is assumed this would apply to the demanding office of Secretary also.)

2. Should "in-kind" gifts be considered?

    Mrs. Archer has, on several occasions, reminded the group that while it had been a pleasure to host the Board's Christmastime dinner at her lovely home, it was still an expense which her husband's tax deduction hadn't begun to cover. Mr. Shapiro told her that on that basis, he hoped the flowers the Board had sent had been treated as income.

    The resulting exchange was ruled off the record, but it led to a suggestion that the Board clarify its liability coverage.

Mr. Russell gave his regular speech about harmony and the joy of working together in a great crusade. (Please see any previous minutes for exact wording.)

After a cooling-off break, Mr. Widen continued his fundraising report. He said there had been a few other setbacks. The telethon had turned out to compete with an unexpected seventh game of the World Series. To compound the problem, it had been carried on a cable channel not yet hooked up in our town (but several people as far away as Charles County had said it came through loud and clear). The net loss was $9,828.41. Though the Fundraising Drive Head described the total as a disappointment, he felt that the experience and exposure would stand the association in good stead. He also said we may want to consider expanding to Charles County to take advantage of the softening up already accomplished there.

The door-to-door campaign had run into a discouraging obstacle. Mr. Widen and his campaign advisers had given long and careful consideration to the choice of a time when absolutely the most people would be at home, and they had been fortunate to get a permit for that very day. Mr. Widen indicated with some pride that obviously no one else had been alert enough to come up with the idea. The only down side and disappointing aspect was that they had never in this world believed that 95 percent of their volunteers would be so disloyal as to also stay home on Super Bowl Sunday. The net loss was $13,870.

Mr. Widen summarized that all in all it hadn't been nearly as good a year as hoped. He said that perhaps in the remaining two months they would be able to try some additional gimmicks. Mrs. Greenlaw said that she didn't think the association could afford any more fundraising.

Mrs. Lortz asked permission to bring up a timely matter and, with the Chair's assent, reintroduced her stale idea for an auxiliary. This time she emphasized the favorable fundraising role that other auxiliaries play for their organizations. With that comment, several board members became rigidly alert. Mrs. Lortz said that there were certain ironclad rules necessary for the success of an auxiliary that, if followed, could result in thousands, and eventually, maybe millions of dollars for the association. She said that if this organization would provide the seed money to set up the auxiliary and would allow the auxiliary to be totally autonomous, she could guarantee results and might even be willing to head it herself. Mr. Gonzalez asked if the income of the auxiliary could go to the association, and the answer was decidedly affirmative, but only after the auxiliary's own projects were fully funded and endowed.

Mr. Goldberg asked what the auxiliary would do. Mrs. Lortz responded that it would have its own bylaws, officers, board, bank accounts, and as soon as possible, staff and office. "But what would it do?" Mr. Colbert persisted. Mrs. Lortz explained that until the auxiliary was established and its officers and board put in place, it would be inappropriate to speak for them.

The matter of an auxiliary was tabled.

Mr. Russell said it was time for committee reports.

He, himself, reported for the Executive Committee, saying only that they had met eleven times since the last board meeting and had worked very hard on behalf of the Board. Mrs. Archer asked if he could give some examples of what they had been doing, but Mr. Russell explained that because the Executive Committee deals with so many sensitive matters, its meetings have to be off the record. He apologized but indicated that, as experienced volunteers, he was sure they would understand.

Mr. Scala asked who was on the Executive Committee, but was told the list is secret. He was assured that many of its members were present at the table at that very moment. A tingle shot through the room. Mrs. Buckminster asked if the Executive Committee had conducted an annual evaluation of Mr. Neal's performance. Mr. Russell said he would not be revealing a confidence to say that they had, but that he could not say more than that. Mrs. Buckminster probed to learn what the Executive Secretary's current salary was. Her brashness was greeted by gasps from the older members.

A few inexperienced board members joined in going beyond the appropriate authority and asked for at least the general salary range. In a spirit of cooperation and camaraderie, Mr. Russell said that although he could not answer the question directly, he would give the Board three guesses. "Under $100,000?" asked Archer. "Yes," said Russell. ("Thank God," said Colberg.)

"Does the figure we're talking about include benefits?" asked Zukert. "Yes," said Russell, but added, "That's question two." "Foul," cried Zukert.

"Is it between $20,000 and $50,000?" asked Knight. "Generally," said Russell.

And just before he closed discussion, Greenlaw queried, "Next time, can we play twenty questions?"

In the absence of the Vice-Chairperson, Mrs. Mitchell (who has missed 3 out of the last 5 meetings, 6 of the last 10, and 19 out of 30), Mr. Shapiro gave the report of the Personnel Committee.

The Board referred to them the disagreement between the Executive Secretary and Mrs. Mitchell over who should approve sick leave. The Committee, recognizing that Mrs. Mitchell has had much more personnel experience than the Executive Secretary, recommended that all personnel decisions reside with her.

Because of the sensitivity of the issue, the staff was asked to leave the room and the Board quickly approved the Committee report. (While in executive session, the Board also voted to move the office, give a raise to "great old Paula," and revise the letterhead.)

The Committee also reported on its position on maternity leave. They said that because the current staff were all over forty, with the exception of Beverly, the one-day-a-week bookkeeper-Dictaphone transcriber-telephone operator and general handy person who had already just had a baby, there was no need for a policy and therefore the matter had been tabled. The Board approved but said that should anyone get pregnant, the matter should come up again. Mr. Zukert said that when the issue is discussed the idea of coverage for paternity should also be considered. Mrs. O'Reilly snapped that if a man is involved in paternity, the association has no obligation whatsoever, and the matter was dropped.

There was a brief report of the Annual Meeting committee. The Governor had been invited to speak but so far no answer had been received. Because the day was getting closer we needed to have a backup. Mrs. Greenlaw pointed out that this was exactly the same situation the organization had faced ten years in a row and that the Governor hadn't showed up yet. Mr. Knight pointed out that this year the Governor is a Republican. Mrs. Scala wanted to know, "What the hell does that have to do with his showing up?" Mr. Knight said it was generally recognized that Republicans are more responsible. Mr. Russell reminded the group once again that we were nonpartisan.

When the group considered a substitute, just in case the Republican Governor didn't show up, it was obvious that we should turn once again to our Founder, First Chairperson, and Chairman Emeritus, who was persuaded to stand in for the Governor. This would be the tenth year in a row that our community would have an opportunity to learn of the founding and earliest days of our association. When discussion turned to an award for the speaker, Mr. Peter Paul Henderson discreetly left the room. In his absence, it was agreed that we would have the plaque made up for the Governor but ask Hardy's Sport Shop to be ready to switch the simulated brass plate on the award at the last minute.

The next report was from the Bylaws Committee with Ms. Trister reporting for Mr. Fales who was absent (due to personal circumstances—different from the personal circumstances that kept him from the last meeting).

The Committee presented its seventeenth draft of the proposed Bylaws revisions, now stretching over four and one-half years of study. At the Board's last meeting, some had objected to the language of proposed amendments to Article XXCVI, Section 78c (Removal of Committee Members) because it might have been construed to provide a committee chairperson with arbitrary authority to dismiss members who were consistently in the minority.

The new revised proposal included a new phrase: "Consistent losers, no matter how often on the wrong side, are protected by due process." To underscore this point, the Committee had added a parenthetical phrase: "This sacred institution, under God, shall neither be ruled by the tyranny of the majority nor the tyranny of the minority."

That amendment, as revised, was officially moved and seconded. During discussion, it was pointed out that the use of the term "minority" could be misread and that therefore it was moved to add the word "numerical" in front of both "minority" and "majority" wherever they appear. The motion to amend the revised amendment to the Bylaws was seconded.

Ms. Trister reminded the Board that the Bylaws Committee had spent two evenings crafting this revised language and that she was not sure she and Mr. Fales could hold the committee together much longer if the Board continued to behave like a board of editors rather than a board of directors—and on that basis she flatly rejected any such amendment. Several members applauded.

Mr. Widen sympathized with the Bylaws Committee, but said that in the spirit of democracy, Bylaws should reflect the will of the governed. Several members clapped (including two who already had applauded the previous speaker). In that larger spirit, Mr. Widen offered an amendment to the amendment to the revised amendment to the Bylaws, which read, "Minorities reflected by numbers, race, ethnic origin, gender, sexual preference, or Christian denomination."

Mr. Zukert pointed out that not all religions are Christian, and, therefore, she moved that in the amendment to the amendment to the revised amendment to the Bylaws, "Christian denomination" be struck. In that same spirit, Mrs. Lortz moved that in the parenthetical section, the phrase beginning, "This sacred institution, under God. . ." be dropped because it flew in the face of separation of church and state. Mr. Widen agreed to accept her suggestion as part of his motion, but the seconder to Mr. Widen's motion did not, and, therefore, Mrs. Lortz asked that as a matter of principle, she, as a Christian herself, be the one to move that the whole parenthetical clause be stricken.

A howl of protest erupted. Rev. Horsinger offered a Solomon-like solution in the form of a substitute motion which proposed that in the amendment to the amendment to amend the revised Bylaws, instead of striking the words "Christian denomination," the word "religion" be substituted. Mrs. O'Reilly shouted that she sympathized wholly with Rev. Horsinger's intent, but that it left a loophole wide enough for the devil himself to drive through. She asked if he would accept an amendment to his substitute motion so that instead of just "religion" the phrase would be: "God-fearing religions, definitely not including some of the new weirdo cults." There was strong applause. Before Rev. Horsinger could reply, Mrs. Lortz was on her feet demanding that everybody was out of order until her motion for precedence could be addressed.

To bring order to the chaos, the more experienced George Horton moved the previous question, but his intent was frustrated when Lucas Zukert asked which of the nine previous questions he was talking about. Pandemonium prevailed.

Finally, Ms. Greenlaw, shouting louder than the others, demanded a point of personal privilege and when recognized said, "I move that I'm lost." Mr. Scala asked if she would accept an amendment so that it would say, "We are all lost" and said authoritatively that *Robert's Rules* gave this motion the highest order. Mrs. Lortz challenged whether a motion that "We are all lost" had a higher standing than a motion for highest precedence, and Mr. Horton assured her it did.

Ms. Trister said that because this item was only the first of sixteen recommendations of the Bylaws Committee to be considered by the Board that evening, she hoped that the Board would be willing for her to take all of these ideas back to the Committee and to come forward at another meeting with a proposal incorporating all of the various motions and ideas. Mr. Widen said if they could do that, they could leave God in wherever they wanted.

The Chairperson said that unraveling all these motions would have to start with the person who made the last motion being willing to be the first to back off so that the matter could be referred back to the Committee and so forth down through each of the people who had made a motion. Mrs. O'Reilly said she would obstruct the process unless she was guaranteed that a Catholic would be added to the Bylaws Committee. In the interest of peace and sanity, Mr. Russell guaranteed that every person who had made a motion had a right to be certain that an individual of his or her political, philosophical, religious, or sexual preference would be represented on the Bylaws Committee. On that basis, the unraveling proceeded.

Ms. Trister announced that the second item the Bylaws Committee was bringing before the Board related to whether the organization should use the term Chairman, Chairwoman, Chairperson, or Chair. Before she could offer her first motion, Mr. Russell gave the Board its choice of a recess, adjournment, or dissolution and fled the room.

On reconvening, the Chairperson said that in the interest of a change of pace, he was taking the privilege of moving ahead to the idea of having a "Board Retreat." Mrs. Zukert kicked off the discussion about a one- or two-day "retreat" when all the board members would go off together to some secluded place to have a good block of uninterrupted time to really think about the state of the association and to get to know each other better. Mr. Knight was concerned that his wife would be terribly upset about his participating in such a co-ed venture. Ms. Greenlaw said his wife had no idea how safe she was.

Mr. Shapiro wanted to know what exactly would be accomplished during a retreat. Mr. Zukert pointed out that all of the Board's regular meetings were so taken up with the kind of important matters we had been discussing that evening that there was never a chance to really "brainstorm" or engage in "blue skying." Mrs. Archer wanted to know how you got that kind of a process going and Mr. Zukert indicated that most often it just starts with people talking off the top of their heads. Mrs. Archer reacted by saying that that was not something this group needs to go away for two days to get good at.

Mrs. Zukert asked the group to put aside immediate considerations and to try to see the idea from the point of view of the board members getting to know each other's strengths and weaknesses. Mr. Gonzalez said that might be pressing our luck.

Ignoring these immediate doubts about the process, Mr. Zukert asked the group where such a session might be held. Four locations were suggested, but the reactions were so violently divided that Mr. Zukert concluded that a group that couldn't decide on the location for a "retreat" probably wasn't ready for one.

The final report for this meeting was by the Evaluation Committee and was presented by Mrs. Buckminster. She pointed out that the Committee deliberately included some "hard-nosed businessmen," as well as a number of social scientists and others who were used to getting to "the heart of the matter." She assured the Board that the language of the committee was laced with such concrete terms as "bottom line," "cost-effectiveness," and "management by objectives," and that this was one evaluation where just doing good was not good enough. For example, she said that one of the businessmen had been particularly helpful in pointing out that our program of public education would always defy quantitative analysis and therefore we should drop any pursuits that can't be measured in specific body counts.

Rev. Horsinger interjected that it was wrong for a voluntary organization to sell its soul for the sake of doing something just because it can be measured. Mrs. Buckminster responded by asking the Reverend why he thought the Girl Scouts sell cookies.

Mr. Colberg said that if the churches had more doers and fewer worshippers, or more sales than prayers, there would be a more business-like approach to God and a lot more souls could be saved per minister. The Reverend seemed moved by this admonition and asked what specific ideas there might be to implement the idea. Mr. Colberg said he couldn't be specific but there was no doubt in his mind that all churches and other nonprofit organizations with all their bleeding heart do-gooders would be much better off if the people working in them had MBA degrees rather than their abstract training in divinity, archeology, social work, or library science. He capped his point by asking, "How many Bibles has theology ever sold?"

Mr. Russell asked what this hard-nosed Committee had concluded and Mrs. Buckminster said that the findings of their two-year evaluation could be summarized as follows: "Any organization made up of such bright people, who are so dedicated and who have worked so hard, must be doing a great deal of good."

Some Board members wept.

On that positive note, the meeting was adjourned at 11:16 P.M.

> Respectfully submitted,
> Mrs. Jeffrey (Effi) Black
> Secretary of the Board of Directors

Attested:
Brian O'Connell
October 26, 2002

References of Books and Articles Cited in Text

AAFRC Trust for Philanthropy
Giving USA 2002: The Annual Report on Philanthropy for the Year 2001. New York: AAFRC Trust for Philanthropy, 2002.

Adult Education Association of the U.S.A.
"Better Boards and Committees." Washington, DC: American Education Association of the U.S.A., 1957.

American Institute of Certified Public Accountants (AICPA)
Not-for-Profit Organizations – AICPA Audit and Accounting Guide. New York, 2002.

Anthony, Robert N., and Regina E. Herzlinger
Management Control in Nonprofit Organizations. Homewood, IL: Richard D. Irwin, Inc., 1975.

Axelrod, Nancy
    A Guide for New Trustees. Washington, DC: Association of Governing Boards of Universities and Colleges, 1982.

Barry, Brian W.
    Strategic Planning Workbook for Nonprofit Organizations. Minnesota: Amherst H. Wilder Foundation, 1997.

BBB Wise Giving Alliance
    "Standards for Charitable Accountability." Virginia, 2002.

Channing L. Bete Co., Inc.
    "The A-B-C's of Parliamentary Procedure." South Deerfield, MA, revised 1998.

Church, David M.
    How to Succeed with Volunteers. New York: National Public Relations Council of Health and Welfare Services, Inc., 1962.

Cleary, Robert E.
    "Something Personal About It." *AGB Reports* 22, 2 (March/April 1980) pp. 38–42.

Conference Board
    Across the Board (March/April 1989). Vol. XXVI, No. 3, pp. 24–31.

Curti, Merle
    "American Philanthropy and the National Character." *American Quarterly* 10 (Winter 1958): pp. 420-437.

Dorsey, Eugene C.
    "The Role of the Board Chairperson." Washington, DC: BoardSource, 1992.

Drucker, Peter
    "Managing the Third Sector." *Wall Street Journal* (October 3, 1978).

Drucker, Peter
    "What Business Can Learn from Nonprofits." *Harvard Business Review* 68, 4, (July–August 1989).

Gale, Robert L.
  Building a More Effective Board. Washington, DC: Association of Governing Boards of Universities and Colleges, 1984.

Gardner, John W.
  "The Independent Sector," in *America's Voluntary Spirit,* compiled by Brian O'Connell. New York: The Foundation Center, 1983.

Hardy, James M.
  Managing for Impact of Nonprofit Organizations: Corporate Planning Techniques and Applications. Erwin, TX: Essex Press, 1984.

Herzberg, Frederick
  "The Motivation to Work," in *Work and the Nature of Man*. New York: Thomas Y. Crowell, 1966.

Houle, Cyril O.
  Governing Boards. San Francisco, CA: Jossey-Bass Publishers, 1989.

INDEPENDENT SECTOR
  "Ethics and the Nation's Voluntary and Philanthropic Community: Obedience to the Unenforceable." Washington, DC, 1991, revised 2003.

INDEPENDENT SECTOR
  Giving and Volunteering in the United States: Findings from a National Survey, 2001 Edition. Washington, DC, 2002.

Irwin, Inez Haynes
  "The Last Days of the Fight for Women's Suffrage," in *The Story of Alice Paul and the National Woman's Party*. Fairfax, VA: Denlingers Publishers Ltd., 1964.

Knauft, E.B., Renee Berger, and Sandra T. Gray
  Profiles of Excellence: Achieving Success in the Nonprofit Sector. San Francisco, CA: Jossey-Bass Publishers, 1991.

Lang, Andrew S., CPA
  "Financial Responsibility of the Nonprofit Board." Washington, DC: BoardSource, 1998.

Lippincott, Earle, and Elling Aannestad
"How Can Businessmen Evaluate the Management of Voluntary Welfare Agencies?" *Harvard Business Review* 42,6 (November–December 1964): p. 870.

Mirvis, Phillip, and Edward Hackett
"Work and Workforce Characteristics in the Non-profit Sector." *The Monthly Labor Review* (April 1983).

National Charities Information Bureau
The Volunteer Board Member in Philanthropy. New York: National Charities Information Bureau, 1968.

National Health Council, National Assembly of National Voluntary Health and Social Welfare Organizations, and United Way of America
Standards of Accounting and Financial Reporting for Voluntary Health and Welfare Organizations. Washington, DC: National Health Council, revised November 1998.

Nielsen, Waldemar A.
The Endangered Sector. New York: Columbia University Press, 1979.

O'Connell, Brian
America's Voluntary Spirit. New York: The Foundation Center, 1983.

Payton, Robert L.
"Major Challenges to Philanthropy." Washington, DC: INDEPENDENT SECTOR, 1984.

Peters, Thomas J., and Robert H. Waterman, Jr.
In Search of Excellence: Lessons from America's Best Run Companies. New York: Harber & Row, 1982.

Plinio, Alex, and JoAnne Scanlan
"Resource Raising: The Role of Non-Cash Assistance in Corporate Philanthropy." Washington, DC: INDEPENDENT SECTOR, 1986.

Price Waterhouse
   The Audit Committee: The Board of Trustees of Nonprofit Organizations and the Independent Accountant. New York: Price Waterhouse, 1980.

Robert, Henry M., III, William J. Evans, Daniel H. Honemann, and Thomas J. Balch
   Robert's Rules of Order Newly Revised, 10th Edition. New York, NY: Perseus Books Group, 2000.

Savage, Thomas J., S.J.
   Seven Steps to a More Effective Board. Boston, MA: The Cheswick Center, revised May 1994.

Selby, Cecily Cannan
   "Better Performance from Nonprofits." *Harvard Business Review* 56, 5 (September/October 1978): pp. 77–83.

Smith, David Horton
   "Evaluating Nonprofit Activity," in *The Nonprofit Organization Handbook,* edited by Tracy D. Connors. New York: McGraw-Hill, 1980.

Szanton, Peter
   "Evaluation and the Nonprofit Board." Washington, DC: BoardSource, revised 1998.

Toppe, Christopher, and Arthur D. Kirsch
   "Keeping the Trust: Confidence in Charitable Organizations in an Age of Scrutiny." Washington, DC: INDEPENDENT SECTOR, 2002.

Washington, Booker T.
   "Raising Money," in *Up from Slavery: An Autobiography, 1901. Reprinted in America's Voluntary Spirit,* compiled by Brian O'Connell. New York: The Foundation Center, 1983.

Weber, Joseph
   Managing the Board of Directors. New York: Greater New York Fund, Inc., 1975.

Wilson, E.B.

"Committee on Trustees." Washington, DC: Association of Governing Boards of Universities and Colleges, 2001.

Zwingle, J.L.

"Conflict in the Board Room." *AGB Reports* 23, 4 (July/August 1981): pp. 23–32.

Index